MO]

BROOKLYN GANGSTERS
70 SQUARE MILES OF BLOOD AND BALLS

CONTRIBUTORS

Kristina DiMatteo
Nick Christophers
Sonny Girard
Joe Bruno
Ed Lieber
Carol Torres
Matthew DiMatteo

CONTENTS

Introduction..4
Preface..7
Alphonse Capone..11
Frankie Yale...20
Abraham Reles...27
Louis Buchalter..35
Benjamin Siegel...43
Albert Anastasia..54
Giuseppe Carlo Bonanno..................................63
Paul Vario...71
Roy DeMeo..78
Anthony Casso..86
Dominick Napolitano..96
John Joseph Gotti..103
Louis Capone...115
Seymour Magoon...118
Harry Strauss...122
Louis Amberg..126
Albert Ackalitis...129
Salvatore Musacchio.......................................133
Alphonse Frank Tieri......................................137
Joseph Colombo..140
Anthony Augello...143
Richard Pagliarulo..146

INTRODUCTION TO BROOKLYN GANGSTERS
By Nick Christophers

Through history we have been introduced to and fascinated by the existence of what has become known as the "Mafia". This organization has spanned generations and has become a fabric of everyday life in key locations around the globe. There have been books, encyclopedias, movies and recently ring tones related to the subject. We would like to introduce this element under a different light.

The origin of this 'brotherhood" was set in motion in the scenic yet tragic island of Sicily. But it spread its tentacles across the world reaching many major cities to plant its flags. One of those major cities is Brooklyn, New York. This specific location became the birthplace to many mobsters and an area where mobsters abroad would eventually call their home.

Yet one must understand that the criminal element was not solely Sicilian but made up of many ethnicities (Irish, Jewish, Greek, Polish, Russian etc.). The theory that the "Mafia" is only Italian is obviously a falsehood.

In reality the first criminal element that rose in the earlier years of American history were predominantly Irish and Jewish. The Irish, in particular in Brooklyn, did not welcome the Italians as they came to settle in their tight knit neighborhoods. They not only dominated law enforcement but also the criminal element at the time. Hence, they did everything they could to make the strangers feel unwelcome.

One example was even documented in the New York Times: "The ill-feeling which has long existed between the Irish and Italian denizens of the tenements in Mulberry-street, between Canal and Hester streets, culminated last evening in a street conflict which at one time assumed serious proportions, and but for the prompt arrival of a strong police force would have resulted in loss of life."

This was evident not only in New York but in any of the major cities at that turn of the century. A man by the name of John Vallone described some of his experience. "But that there was considerable misunderstanding of the true character of the new immigrant cannot be overlooked or denied. The discrimination against him was at times mean and low and inexcusable. By word and conduct he was treated as inferior. This was particularly true of the treatment he received from the Irish."

In the early 1900's many various immigrants entered the already bustling borough of Brooklyn, and each one experienced some kind of discrimination. Whether it was the Italians, Jews, Greeks or even the Irish, they all suffered some mistreatment. An example of this was depicted in the blockbuster film "Gangs Of New York" directed by Martin Scorcese that highlighted the birth of street gangs (Irish against Native Americans).

This fact gave birth to the various clans that sprouted across the borough. A way for these immigrants to escape ill-treatment, they created tight-knit crews that would protect their own. This also introduced the lack of respect for authority especially for the Italians when the majority of the police were Irish. Soon the Sicilians and Calabrians, unlike other ethnic gangs, began painting their outfit with more alluring colors. In this book we will explore one of the key locations where the "Mafia" element flourished. Brooklyn, New York has and always will have an image of toughness and grittiness unmatched anywhere else in the five boroughs. In this book we will offer documented information on how that image came to light.

The borough of Brooklyn has given birth to many characters that have molded the model of the Mafia. Names like Al Capone, Frankie Yale and Anthony Casso are just a few who will be introduced in this publication. Brooklyn, with its brownstones and old fashioned family enclaves, served as a perfect fit for these criminals.

We have been exposed to films that invoke the dark yet flashy life of these individuals. Films like The Lords of Flatbush, Goodfellas, Donnie Brasco, We Own The Night and others have given us a visual into that world. All of these have been based in the borough of Brooklyn.

This publication will highlight a score of mobsters that either shaped the organization or lended a hand in its longevity. In this book we will also offer personal information on each of these individuals that has never been released or embellished. So come with us from Mob Candy Magazine on this bloody road to mob-dom in Brooklyn, New York.

Immigrants arriving at Ellis Island.

Paul Mancino's Focacceria, now Ferdinando's Focacceria at 151 Union Street, Brooklyn.

PREFACE

Even though I met some of the men in this book, I put it together because I'm from Brooklyn and liked the idea of putting something out that showed the link between gangsters and Brooklyn. I always knew it because I was born in it. I had the pleasure to meet and deal with some characters in the mob world that I would not have had the chance to meet if I was a regular guy. I do find it interesting how many guys that I have met that were so passionate and yet would also be so violent. They really believed in what they were doing, whether it was shake downs, scores, murders, or protecting each other and their families and the belief that there was honor among thieves. I've met bosses, capos, made men, consigliere, killers, thieves, money makers, gofers and associates in every family in the mob from Rhode Island to New York to New Jersey. As I sit here now and think, they all had the same idiotic beliefs, loyalty to their bosses and their partners and they thought that this thing of ours would never end. I did meet some that I still respect and some that I think are assholes then and even now. Here is a little of my background. I was born in South Brooklyn in 1956 where my grandfather was a longshoreman. He worked the Brooklyn and New York docks from the 1930's till the late 1960's. He met most gangsters that ran the docks but would not get involved with the life.

My father was the bodyguard for Larry Gallo, the boss of the Gallo family, up until Larry died in 1968 of cancer. Growing up with mob guys was a common thing, and on weekends the guys would come to my house to socialize with my father. Guys like Joe Schipani, Larry Gallo, my godfather Bobby Darrow, Albert Gallo, and Nicky Bianco would be there one weekend; the next weekend would be Robert DiBernardo (DeBe), Jimmie Rotundo, and so on. I got a good sense of the life. As I got older I became my father's left hand man. Anything that had to be done I did it for 37 years; we were a team, but he was the power. I just want to tell you some of the bullshit that you go through. My father called me down to speak to Aniello Dellacroce at a sit-down at Toto Marino's Dixie Tavern. Aniello wanted to speak to me. He asked me if I had told this wannabe that "I don't give a fuck who you're with" when, during our argument, said he had said he was with Aniello. I told Aniello that I didn't exactly say that. Aniello knew I was full of shit but gave me a pass because of my father, then told me I was right and that I should have just cracked the asshole. But in that world you can be right and your mouth can make you wrong.

Saying "I don't give a fuck who you're with" is disrespecting Aniello, which wasn't the case, but there are rules and regulations (by the way the guy that made the complaint to Aniello got a crack in the face, was told not to use Aniello's name and got chased from the neighborhood). It's funny how things work. Although I learned a lesson, at seventeen you forget fast. Months later I was on Court Street at an arcade my father and I owned. One day I was watching the place, and there were guys coming in and out. One of them must have been smoking pot outside, so Sally Balsamo comes running in yelling at me. Then I said, "Who the fuck you yelling at and calm down". Sally was a soldier in the same Gallo family my father was in and a lot older than me. He also owned the car service on Court Street and made a ton of money. So down I go to Blast's club thinking, "here I go again". Blast asked me what happened. I told him that I was in the arcade and some assholes must have been outside smoking pot. Sally came running in, yelling at me. I yelled back at him and he got mad. Blast told me I had a right to defend myself, but Sally was older and a big money earner, so I had to go back to the car service and apologize to him. I did, and Sally told me it was okay and that he just didn't want no heat coming down. We stayed good friends right up to his death. I sat down that night at a bar on Court and Atlantic Ave. called the Court Terrace owned by a Gallo associate Rocky T and said to myself "What bullshit; you're right and you're wrong. What the fuck? I better learn the rules or I'm fucked". So I started to stay with my father more often just listening to him teach. I knew if I was there he would teach, and teach he did. We both made it in and out of the mob life. Because my father Ricky was a crazy, old school tough guy, they phased him out. They knew he was a real man and they just wanted flunkies, rats and junkies. And me, I went where my father went. That's a book alone. So 37 years later I sat down and here is what you get, Mob Candy's Brooklyn Gangsters.

Hope you enjoy the read!

- **Uncle Frankie**

Frank and his wife Emily, on Court Street and Douglass Street in 1973.

The Brooklyn Bridge is one of the oldest suspension bridges in the United States. Completed in 1883, it connects the New York City borough of Manhattan and Brooklyn by spanning the East River. With a main span of 1,595.5 feet (486.3 m), it was the longest suspension bridge in the world from its opening until 1903, and the first steel-wire suspension bridge.

A very young Al Capone.

Alphonse Capone
January 17, 1899 - January 25, 1947

ALPHONSE CAPONE
THE FIRST DAPPER DON

His parents came from Naples, Italy in 1893 for a better life, and little did they know their son would take the phrase a 'better life' literately to a different level.

Alphonse Capone's parents were Gabriele (December 12, 1864 – November 14, 1920) and Teresina Capone (December 28, 1867 – November 29, 1952). His father Gabriele was a barber from Castellamarre di Stabia, a town about 16 miles south of Naples, and his mother Teresina was a seamstress and the daughter of Angelo Raiola from Angri, a town in the province of Salerno.

Gabriele and Teresina had nine children: Alphonse "Scarface Al" Capone, James (also known as Richard "Two-Gun" Hart), Rafaelle also known as Ralph "Bottles" Capone (who was later placed in charge of Al Capone's beverage industry), Salvatore "Frank" John, Albert, Matthew, Rose and Mafalda Capone (later Mrs. John J. Maritote).

The Capone family immigrated to the United States in 1893 and settled down at 95 Navy Street, in the Navy Yard section of downtown Brooklyn, near the Barber Shop that employed Gabriele at 69 Park Ave.

On January 17, 1899, nearly six years after they settled in Brooklyn, Alphonse Capone was born.

95 Navy Street, in the Navy Yard section of downtown Brooklyn, near the Barber Shop that employed Gabriele at 69 Park Ave. where Al was born.

The apartment Al lived in had a potbelly stove for heat and the sink was in the hallway. The bathroom was outdoors, hence the term 'back house'. They then moved to an apartment at 69 Park Ave above Gabriele's Barber Shop. Soon after that they settled at 21 Garfield Place, the Red hook section of Brooklyn.

Al attended Public School # 7 located on Adams Street and then moved onto Public School # 133 on Butler Street & 4th Avenue.

He dropped out of school in the the 6th grade at the age of 14. He then began hanging out in the neighborhood. He was known to play pool at Pop's poolroom on Court Street in Red Hook. (A guy from Union Street took the pool table when Pop's was closing in the 80's and still has it today.) Al and his father also used to play pool at a poolroom on 20 Garfield Place.

Al's life in the 'life' began to take root....now.

Not far from Al's home was Johnny Torrio's Association Club. Torrio's club was on 4th Avenue and Union Street. This is where Al would cement his friendship with Johnny and where his schooling began on "street life". He started running errands for Torrio

Besides running errands and getting acquainted in the "life", he also had a legitimate job at a munitions company. He was a paper cutter and earned three to four dollars a week. Al also worked at a candy store at 305 5th Avenue in Brooklyn.

21 Garfield Place, the Red hook section of Brooklyn. The apartment Al lived in.

Johnny Torrio's Association Club. Torrio's club was on 4th Avenue and Union Street.

Al was known for his good taste in clothes and his love for dancing. He would attend a dance hall called the Broadway Casino and the Adonis Club on 12th Street off 3rd Avenue in Red Hook.

He was involved with three street gangs: The Navy Street Boys, Brooklyn Rippers and the Forty Thieves Juniors, where Johnny Torrio and Lucky Luciano were members also. He soon would join the Five Points gang, the "big boy" crew from New York City and help Frankie Yale at his club the Harvard Inn.

Capone was instrumental in aiding Yale by ridding the waterfront of their opponents....the Irish White Handers. Al's first order working for Yale was to pick up some money that was owed to Frankie from Tony Perotta, a fellow tough guy.

It didn't turn out the way it should have, so Al whacked Tony Perotta. When Frankie Yale found out, he wasn't happy about it. Frankie didn't get the $1,500 owed to him but he did like that Al took the gangster way and did a piece of work and that was a feather in Capone's hat.

On one occasion on Christmas Day in 1925, there was an incident at Adonis Social Club in Brooklyn where a few "White Handers" including Richard "Pegleg" Lonegran were gunned down after racial slurs were exchanged.

Undocumented accounts place six Irish gangsters hanging out at the club, when a few Irish girls and their Italian dates arrived. The look of Italian men with Irish girls fueled the Irish gangsters' rage and arguments ensued. After awhile the lights went out and shots were fired.

Only one Irish hood 'James Hart' survived the incident, and he would not divulge exactly what occurred. However, the shooting was soon attributed to Capone and Frankie Yale.

Capone would soon earn his infamous name "Scarface" while working at the Harvard Inn. Late one evening at the bar, his brashness showed its face and he ended up insulting a patron which ended up in a scuffle with the patron's brother. The patron's brother was Frank Galluccio, a known mobster about town.

Al essentially told Frank's sister Lena that she had a "great ass" which ignited Frank to lunge at Al. Frank would pull out a pocketknife and slash Al's face.

Al wanted revenge but was told by the gangster leader Lucky Luciano and crew that Frank was in the right to defend his sister's honor.

Frank and Al would reconcile and the case was closed.

Frank Gallucio, the man responsible for giving Al his infamous name "Scarface".

Capone would meet Mae and eventually have a son named Sonny. Three weeks after Sonny was born Al married Mary (Mae) Coughlin on December 30, 1918. They would wed at St. Mary Star of the Sea on Court Street in the Red Hook section of Brooklyn. Al and his family attended St. Michael's Church near the Navy yard in Brooklyn but Mae's family lived on Court Street and Third Place so they chose to use her parish. St. Mary's also wasn't as strict as St. Michael's; they didn't ask as many questions, like Al's age.

St. Mary Star of the Sea on Court Street in the Red Hook section of Brooklyn.

St. Michael's Church near the Navy yard in Brooklyn, where Al's family went to church.

Al and his new family would move to Baltimore where he would work as a bookkeeper for a construction company of a friend to try to stay away from the gangster way of life.

Johnny Torrio had to leave for Chicago on Black Hand business where members of that group were harassing his sister's husband. Al came back from Baltimore to Brooklyn when his father died on November 14, 1920, from a heart attack at the pool room on Garfield place. Al would soon be summoned to Chicago to help his boss Johnny Torrio. The Black Handers were dealt with accordingly.

15 - Brooklyn Gangsters

While Al settled in Chicago, things took a bad turn with his friend Frankie Yale.

Capone was upset with Yale's refusal to support Antonio Lombardo as leader of the Unione Sicliane. In turn, Yale decided to halt liquor trucks headed for Chicago. This was a problem for Capone and he needed to remedy it. After a hit on Capone's spy James DeAmato, Yale's days were numbered. Capone set up a plan to eliminate his one time employer.

Frankie was lured out of his club in fear that his wife was in danger. He drove back to his home and as he was getting close to home another car drove alongside and let out a burst of bullets that not only killed Frank but caused him to crash just blocks from his home. From then on Capone would later become the dominant force in the Chicago underworld until his arrest for tax evasion in 1931. He would serve 11 years.

Al would serve 11 years for tax evasion.

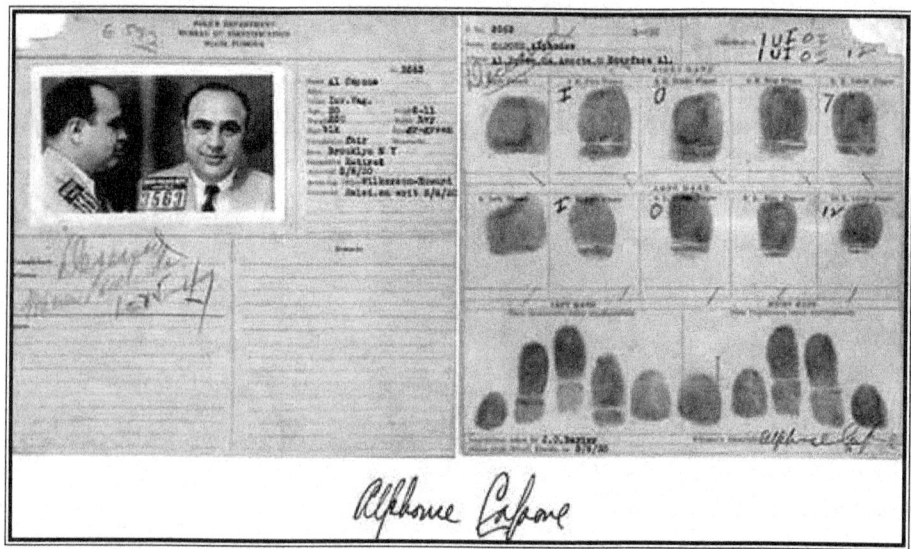

Al's finger prints from his 1930 Miami arrest. Al also served time in Alcatraz.

16 - Brooklyn Gangsters

Frank "The Enforcer" Nitto, known for taking over as the boss of Chicago for Capone, was originally with the The Navy Street Boys in Brooklyn, Al's first street gang, and was known for being a tough street guy with Al Capone.

As a youth Al contracted syphilis, which led to an early and untimely passing. Al died of a stroke while retired in Florida on January 25,1947. Capone was, and always will be, one of the most colorful of American gangsters to date.

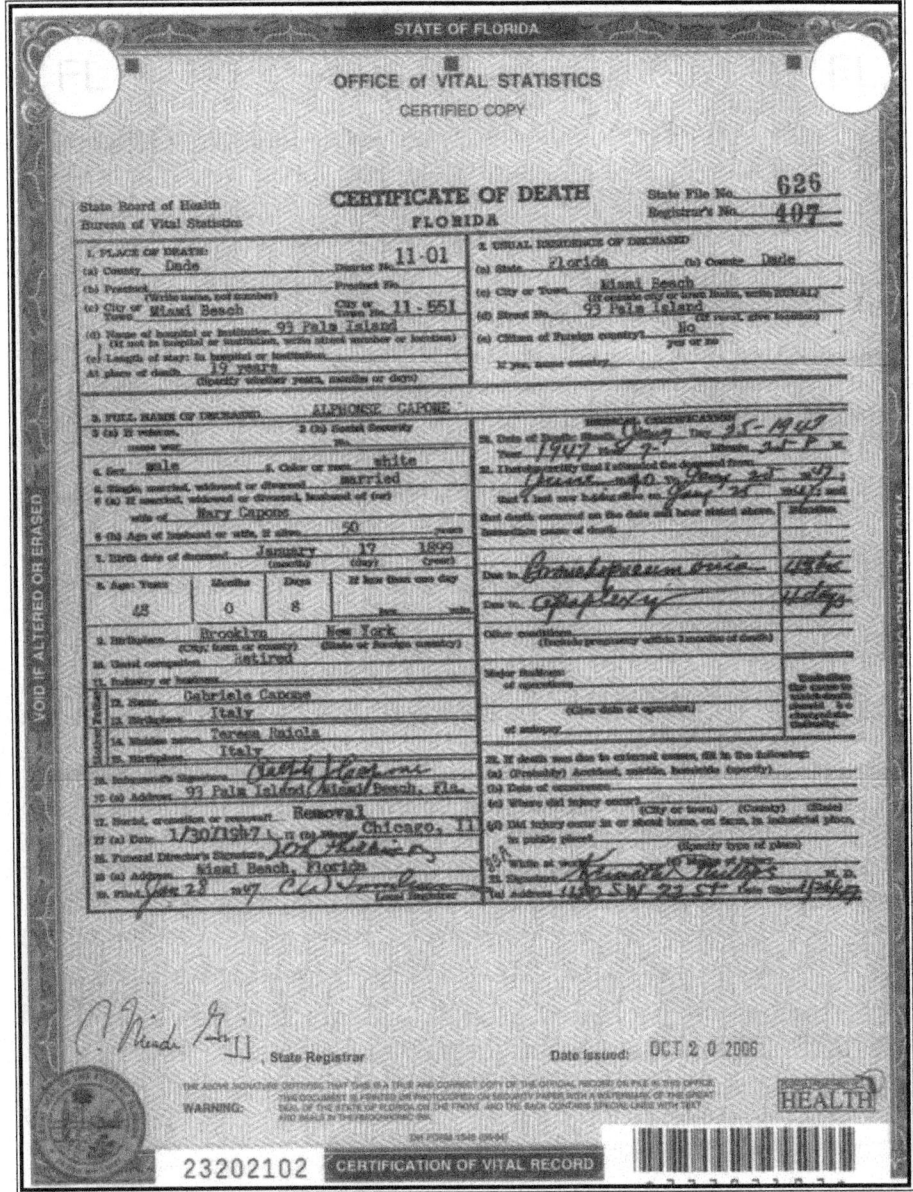

Al would die of a fatal stroke while retired in Florida, January 25, 1947. He was 48.

17 - Brooklyn Gangsters

A Life Magazine article called "Mobsters & Gangsters – From Al Capone to Tony Soprano" indicated that Al was called "Snorky" by his closest friends.

As we all know Al Capone went to Chicago and started a legacy, from the killing of Big Jim Colosimo to O'Banion and his involvement in the St. Valentine's Day Massacre, to his generosity to the hungry with his soup kitchens. Al made his fortune in bootlegging till the end of prohibition. He always had his hand in Brooklyn from booze to the Union Siciliana and the rest is history.

We're also told Capone once said Chicago was a piece of cake compared to Brooklyn, his home.

The Manhattan Bridge is a suspension bridge that crosses the East River in New York City, connecting Lower Manhattan (at Canal Street) with Brooklyn (at Flatbush Avenue Extension). It was the last of the three suspension bridges built across the lower East River, following the Brooklyn and the Williamsburg bridges.

Frankie Yale
January 22, 1893 - July 1, 1928

FRANKIE YALE
PRINCE OF PALS

Frankie Yale, real name Francesco Loele, was the number one mobster in Brooklyn for most of the Roaring Twenties. In 1893, Yale was born in a Calabrian town of Longobucco, in Italy. In 1901, he immigrated to the United States and soon he became involved in a life of crime. Although his stomping grounds were in South Brooklyn, Yale met fellow Brooklynite Johnny Torrio and they became partners. Yale joined Torrio in the Five Points Gang in Lower Manhattan, under the wing of mob boss Paul Kelly.

Torrio and Yale were involved in several illegal endeavors, but their big money maker was a version of the Black Hand extortion shakedown, where they threatened to kill Italian immigrants unless they paid protection money. Most paid, but some didn't. In the gangster world it was known that Yale had killed a dozen times before he reached the age of twenty-one. Yale's gang engaged in Black Hand extortion activities and ran a string of brothels. Their gang was feared by most. It included Italians from all regions and could work in partnership with other ethnic groups if it was good for business. Frankie's "services" to his customers included offering "protection" to local merchants, controlling food services for restaurants, as well as ice deliveries for Brooklyn residents. Yale's notorious sideline was his line of cigars, foul-smelling stogies packaged in boxes that bore his portrait. Frankie also owned and operated his own funeral home at 6604 14th Avenue (he and his family lived across the street). When asked about his profession, Yale stated that he was an "undertaker". In addition to Al Capone, other gangsters who worked under Frankie Yale at one time or another included Vincent Mangano, Joe Adonis, Anthony "Little Augie" Carfano and Albert Anastasia. Yale's top assassin was Willie "Two Knife" Altierri, nicknamed as such due to his method of killing. Yale at age 17, and a friend Bobby Nelson hung out at a pool room in Coney Island. One night they got into a fight with some drunks beating them so badly that they didn't get out of the hospital for weeks. Yale and Nelson had to go on the lam for weeks. As soon as they came back, Yale was arrested. That was not the first time. His first arrest came in 1912 for suspicion of homocide.

Johnny Torrio- Yale joined Torrio in the Five Points Gang in Lower Manhattan.

Frankie Yale had to go on the lam after a fight in a pool room in Coney Island. His first arrest was in 1912 for suspicion of homocide.

21 - Brooklyn Gangsters

Soon after the Harvard Inn opened in 1916 Frankie married Maria Delapia, with whom he would have two daughters, Rosa and Isabella. Yale was also noted as a stylish dresser, favoring expensive suits and diamond jewelry. One newspaper reporter called him the "Beau Brummell of Brooklyn." Frankie was also known for his generosity to the less fortunate in his neighborhood, who, often approached Yale as he sipped coffee in his cafe, requesting financial assistance. After a local deli owner was robbed, Frankie replaced his lost cash. After a fish peddler lost his cart, Yale gave him $200 with an admonishment, "Get a horse, you're too old to walk." Yale was dubbed the "Prince of Pals", known to appreciate funny stories, good food and drink. Yale was a very personable man.

Tradition has long claimed that Frankie Yale fought a desperate gang war for control of the Brooklyn docks with the Irish White Hand Gang. Historians have called much of that into question and indicated that Yale's worst enemies were not the Irish waterfront racketeers, but rival Italian crime families who were constantly jockeying for power in Brooklyn during the 1920's. Although the Irish White Handlers were the gangsters that were running everything in Brooklyn before the Italians got there, Yale had no love for them. They had been fighting for the Docks for years until Yale brought in Capone from Chicago in 1925, and had a showdown with Peg Leg Lonergan at the Adonis Social Club that night. Capone and a few crewmembers had a confrontation with Lonergan, the boss of the White Handlers. When it was over, Lonergan and three crewmembers were dead. That pretty much put an end to the Irish White Hand in South Brooklyn.

The murder scene of Peg Leg Lonergan at Adoni's Social Club.

The first known attempt on Frankie Yale's life occurred on February 6, 1921, when he and two of his men were ambushed in Lower Manhattan after they stepped from their car in order to attend a banquet. One of Yale's bodyguards was killed and the other wounded, with Frankie himself sustaining a severe wound. Frankie would pull through after an extended recovery.

Five months after Frankie's injury, on July 15, 1921, Yale, his brother Angelo, and four men were driving on Cropsey Avenue in Bath Beach, Brooklyn when another car filled with rival gunmen overtook them and opened fire. Angelo and one of Frankie's men were wounded. The attack was believed to have been an act of revenge for the June 5th murder of a Manhattan mobster named Ernesto Melchiorre, who had been gruesomely murdered after a late-night visit to the Harvard Inn. Melchiorre's brother Silvio was believed to have been the driving force behind the unsuccessful attack. A week later, Yale's men gunned down Silvio Melchiorre in front of his Little Italy cafe.

Yet another attempt on Frankie Yale's life took place on August 8, 1923. Frankie's chauffeur, Frank Forte, had taken the Yale family to a christening at a nearby church. While Frankie decided to walk back to his 14th Avenue home, Forte drove Maria Yale and her two daughters back. As the women exited the vehicle, a carload of four gangsters rolled past, mistook Frank Forte for the boss, and pumped him full of bullets.

Torrio and Yale had their base of operations at the Harvard Inn, a bar and brothel in Coney Island Brooklyn from 1916. In 1919. Torrio moved to Chicago to work for his uncle-through-marriage, mob boss Big Jim Colosimo. Yale filled Torrio's absence by hiring a friend of Torrio's, the 19-year old Al Capone, as his main bouncer at the Harvard Inn. In 1920, Torrio decided the time was ripe for Colosimo's death, so he asked his friend Frankie Yale if he could make the trip to Chicago to do the dirty deed. Torrio set Colosimo up by telling him to go to his cafe to receive an illegal shipment of booze. When he got to the cafe, instead of liquor, Colosimo was greeted by a bullet to the head, supplied by the reliable Yale. At one point Torrio summoned Capone to come to Chicago. Torrio's Chicago empire was being threatened by Irish mob boss Dion O'Banion, who ran a flower shop on North State Street. Torrio decided O'Banion had to go too, and figuring his local shooters couldn't get close enough to O'Banion to kill him, he called on Yale again. O'Banion had never met Yale and wouldn't recognize him. In November 1924, Yale entered O'Banion's flower shop and greeted him with a firm handshake. O'Banion tried to pull his hand free, but before he could pull himself away from Yale's death grip, two of Torrio's men, John Scalise and Albert Anselmi, busted into the shop and shot O'Banion to death.

The murder scene of mob boss Big Jim Colosimo. He was set up and gunned down in his own cafe by Yale.

Irish mob boss Dion O'Banion who was killed in his own flower shop by Frankie Yale.

Mob boss Big Jim Colosimo.

23 - Brooklyn Gangsters

In 1925, Torrio was ambushed and shot several times in front of his apartment building. After he recovered from his wounds, he decided to retire from the rackets and he handed over his illegal empire to the 26-year old Capone.

Capone worked a deal with Yale to import his illegal booze from Chicago to New York City, under Yale's protection. Soon Yale got upset that Capone had chosen Tony Lombardo to be in charge of the Unione Siciliana without talking about it with him first. Yale favored another man, Aiello. Yale started to talk bad about Al, Capone got wind of it and kept a eye on Yale. Yale was a mentor to Al as a kid so Yale didn't think Al would send anyone to Brooklyn to whack him. How wrong he was. Capone's trucks were being hijacked before they got to New York City and Capone suspected Yale was the culprit. He sent of one his best men, James DeAmato, to survey the truck-hijacking situation in New York City. Soon, DeAmato sent word back to Capone that Yale was indeed hijacking Capone's trucks, then selling the liquor back to Capone. Six days later, DeAmato was gunned down on a Brooklyn Street.

26 year old Al Capone who sold illegal booze from Chicago to New York to Yale.

Safely in Miami, Florida, Capone sent six of his shooters to New York City by car. On Sunday afternoon, July 1, 1928, Frankie Yale was in his Sunrise Club in Brooklyn when he received a cryptic phone call. The caller said something was wrong with Frankie's new wife Lucy, who was at home looking after their 1year-old daughter. Refusing Joseph Piraino's offer to drive him, Yale dashed out to his brand new, coffee-colored Lincoln coupe and took off up New Utrecht Avenue. At a red light, Frankie saw four hard-eyed men in a Buick sedan staring at him. While Yale's new Lincoln was fashioned with armor plating, the dealer had neglected to bullet-proof the windows. As a result, when the light changed, Yale hit the gas and took off. After a chase up New Utrecht, Frankie swerved west onto 44th Street, with the Buick close behind. Frankie's car was soon overtaken by the Buick, whose occupants riddled the Brooklyn gang boss with submachine gun bullets. After the Lincoln crashed into a brick wall of a brownstone at 923 44th Street, the killers' Buick screeched to a stop. One man jumped from the Buick, ran over to the totaled Lincoln, and emptied a .45 automatic into Yale's head.

Where Frankie Yale finally crashed at 923 44th Street. After the crash one of his killers got out of his car which had chased him to the crash, and emptied a .45 automatic into Yale's head.

Yale had always admired the grandeur of O'Banion's funeral, so he did him one better. Yale's funeral procession attracted 10,000 mourners, and his funeral cost $50,000, including a $15,000 nickel and silver coffin.

The Department of Docks stood on Pier A, Manhattan's southmost Hudson River pier. This utilitarian brick structure was built in 1886; in 1900, a three-story front section and metal siding were added, and in 1919, a clocktower was appended as the nation's first World War I memorial.

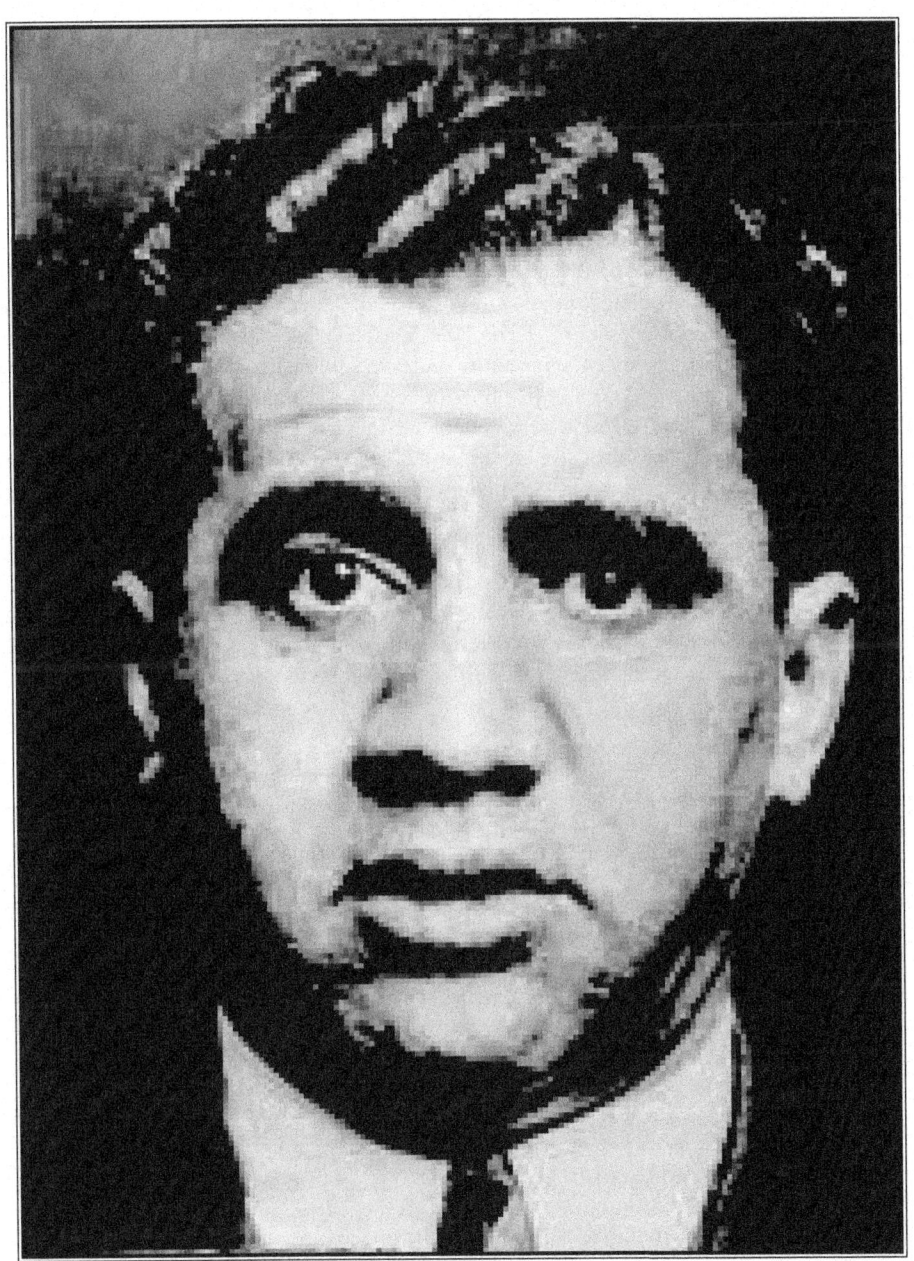

Abraham Reles
May 10, 1906 - November 12, 1941

ABE RELES
KID TWIST

Abraham Reles, the son of Austrian Jewish immigrants Sam Reles and Rose Schulman, was born in the Brownsville section of Brooklyn, New York on May 10, 1906. His father Sam was a tailor. He worked in one of the garment trades until the Great Depression. His father's last known occupation was peddling knishes on the streets of Brownsville. His full formal Hebrew name was "Elkanah Ben Reb Shimon" Reles. Reles married a girl named Lucy and had one son.

The first forty years of the twentieth century saw crime dominated by Italian-American gangs, but that didn't stop those good old Jewish boys in Brooklyn from getting their hands bloodied. They were a crew of "wackos", murderers, and thieves that would go back to their kosher homes at night. Neighborhoods like Brownsville, Ocean Hill and South Brooklyn were all slums with most immigrants living in poverty. It was the only thing the kids knew and the only way out was crime. Poverty was the backbone of crime; either learn how to make money or just stay and let the Irish shit on you.

Reles attended school through the 8th grade. After leaving school, Reles, who stayed on Pitkins Avenue and Watkins Street, began hanging out at Label's poolroom and candy stores in and around Brownsville. He soon teamed up with two of his childhood friends who eventually rose to power with him in the group known as Murder Inc., Martin Goldstein and Harry Strauss.

Martin Goldstein

Harry Strauss

His first arrest came in 1921 at the age of fifteen for stealing $2 worth of gum from a vending machine, and he was sent to a correctional facility upstate for four months. Back at home, Reles and his crew hung out at Midnight Rose's, a storefront on Saratoga Avenue in Brownville, Brooklyn. There he would meet with his crew members and plot future crimes. Upstairs was a Chinese American restaurant called Hollywood-Royal. There they would also plan the next caper. At one point Reles had thirty crew members in and out of Midnight Rose's 24 hours a day. The store never closed. He had Louie Lepke , Louis Capone, Albert Asastasia , Harry "Happy" Maione in for meetings. Rose, at one point, was making a couple of $100,000 a month bookmaking and shylocking for the boys. They figured, " why close ?" . Kid Twist had a long police record, but few convictions. He was charged six times with homicide and never convicted.

28 - Brooklyn Gangsters

Louis Capone.

Harry Strauss, Vito Gurino, Abe Reles, Harry "Happy" Maione.

Midnight Rose's, where Reles had 30 crew members 24 hours a day.

29 - Brooklyn Gangsters

He was arrested nine times on assault charges and had one conviction. Between 1932 and 1940, the lisping gangster was arrested on the average of once every 78 days, but his longest sentence had been two years for assaulting a parking attendant with a bottle. From 1932 to 1934, the law had picked up Kid 23 times but he had spent just 30 days in jail.

Reles was widely considered the most feared hit man for "Murder, Inc.", the enforcement contractor for the National Crime Syndicate. Reles looked like a real gangster. He stood about 5' 5" tall and weighed 160 lbs. with eyes that could scare a dead man. He had a gorilla figure with long arms, hands as big as a catcher's mitt, and a cigarette always hanging from his lip. He was intimidating with a volcanic temper to match.

"Kid Twist's" weapon of choice was an ice pick, which he would ram through his victim's ear into the brain. Reles became good at using the pick but had many others ways to murder.

Reles became known as a particularly cold-blooded and psychopathic murderer. On one occasion, in broad daylight, he attacked a worker at a car wash for failing to clean a smudge from the fender of his car. Another time, Reles killed a parking lot attendant for failing to fetch his car fast enough. On another occasion, he brought a guest to his mother-in-law's home for supper. When his mother-in-law retired after the meal, Reles and another gang member murdered the guest and then removed the body.

Reles got the nickname "Kid Twist" after an earlier New York killer, Max "Kid Twist" Zwerbach. Max was a hood in the "Monk Eastman," a Lower East Side gang. Reles was also a bootlegger who rarely touched alcohol.

During the Prohibition days of the 1920's, while still teenagers, Reles and his friend Martin "Buggsy" Goldstein went to work for the Shapiro brothers, who ran the Brooklyn rackets. Reles, Goldstein, and George Defeo entered the slot machine business in the same area as the Shapiro Brothers. Through Defeo's connections with Meyer Lansky, Reles and Goldstein were able to make a deal with the influential crime lord. Lansky needed access to the poorer neighborhoods of Brooklyn and thus agreed to the deal. Both parties prospered; Lansky was able to get sizeable footholds in Brownsville, East New York, and Ocean Hill, while Reles gained the backing he needed to keep both his business and himself alive. Reles' crew expanded with some new hoods like Louis Tiny Benson, Sholem Bernstein, Julie Catalano, Irving "Gandy" Cohen ,Oscar "The Poet" Friedman, Vito "Socko" Gurino, and lets not forget Abe "Pretty" Levine.

Abe "Pretty" Levine, a man in Reles' crew.

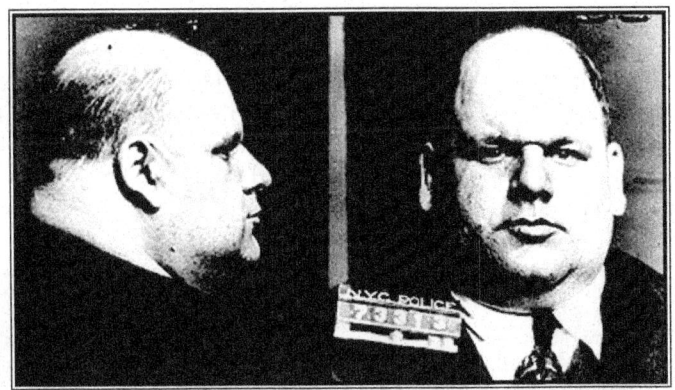

Louis "Tiny" Benson was also in Reles' crew.

Reles, Goldstein and Strauss were partners in all of their criminal activities, which had primarily been the slot machine business, and quickly expanded to include loan sharking, crap games and labor slugging in connection with union activities, especially the "Restaurant Union."

The slot machine business thrived and soon Reles and Goldstein were on the "Shapiros'" hit list. One night, the two men received a phone call from a "friend" saying that the Shapiros had left their East New York headquarters. Hopping into a car with Defeo, they headed to East New York. However, when they reached the Shapiros' building, the three men were ambushed. Reles and Goldstein were wounded, but all three managed to escape. In the meantime, Meyer Shapiro abducted Reles' girlfriend and dragged her to an open field, where he beat and raped her.

Meyer Shapiro, the man who beat and raped Reles' girlfriend in an open field.

To avenge the ambush and his girlfriend's rape, Reles asked the help of fellow crew members Frank "Dasher" Abbandando and Harry "Happy" Maione. By killing the Shapiro brothers, they would take over some of their operations. After several futile attempts by each side to kill the other, the "Murder, Inc." group finally caught up with Irving Shapiro. On that occasion, Reles dragged Irving from the hallway of his home out into the street. Reles beat, kicked, and then shot Irving numerous times, killing him.

31 - Brooklyn Gangsters

Two months later, Reles met Meyer Shapiro on the street and shot him dead in the face. Another three years elapsed before Reles finally got the last Shapiro brother, William. William was abducted off the street and taken to a gang hideout. Once there, William was beaten nearly to death, stuffed into a sack, and driven out to the Canarsie section of Brooklyn and buried. Before the gang could finish burying William, a passerby spotted them and they had to flee the scene. After Shapiro's autopsy, it was determined that he was buried alive.

Frank "Dasher" Abbandando   Abe "Kid Twist" Reles

In 1940, Reles was implicated in a number of killings. Realizing that he faced execution if convicted, Reles became a government witness. Reles implicated his boss in "Murder, Inc," Louis Buchalter, in the murder of Brooklyn candy store owner Joseph Rosen; however, Buchalter was eventually convicted and executed for this crime. Reles' information also implicated Harry "Pittsburgh Phil" Strauss, Mendy Weiss, Harry "Happy" Maione, Frank "Dasher" Abbandando, and even Reles' childhood friend "Buggsy" Goldstein. All of these men were convicted and executed. Following these convictions, Reles' next target was Albert Anastasia, who had been co-chief of operations of "Murder, Inc." Reles was to implicate Anastasia on the murder of union longshoreman Pete Panto. However, unlike other members of "Murder Inc.," Anastasia was a high-ranking member of the Cosa Nostra.

Mendy Weiss

32 - Brooklyn Gangsters

The trial, based solely on Reles' testimony, was set for 12 November 1941. Reles was under constant guard by six police detectives at the Half Moon Hotel on Coney Island. In the early morning of November 12, 1941, Abe Reles fell to his death from a hotel window. It is not known whether he was thrown or pushed out the window, or if he was trying to escape. Allegedly Albert Anastasia and Frank Costello raised $100,000 to bribe police guards to kill Reles. What really got me is how guys of any nationality, Italian, Jewish, Irish and Negro could grow up as kids together and do all these fucked up things. They would kill for looking at them wrong and in the end they cry and send six of their friends to the chair. Why didn't these guys go out in a blaze of glory like James Cagney, not like mutts. Because of his mob status as a "stool pigeon" and the circumstances surrounding his death, Reles gained another moniker after his passing. Reles became known in a newspaper article, as "the canary who sang, but couldn't fly."

Reles is buried in Old Mount Carmel Cemetery in the Glendale section of Queens, New York.

33 - Brooklyn Gangsters

The Soldiers' and Sailors' Memorial Arch, a Civil War memorial designed by John H. Duncan with sculptures by Frederick MacMonnies, stands at Grand Army Plaza in Brooklyn. The arch was built between 1889-92, commemorating Union forces that died in the Civil War. MacMonnies's huge quadriga sculpture on top was installed in 1898, and the two groups on the south pedestals representing the Army and Navy were added in 1901.

Louis Buchalter
February 12, 1897 – March 4, 1944

LOUIS BUCHALTER
LEPKE THE JUDGE

Louis "Lepke" Buchalter (12 February 1897 – 4 March 1944), was the son of Barnett Buchalter who immigrated to the US from Russia. Buchalter's mother's name was Rose. As a result of previous marriages, Lepke was one of eleven children. One of Lepke's brothers became a Rabbi, another a dentist and one sister became a teacher. His father died when Lepke was fourteen in 1911. Louie took the nickname "Lepke" at an early age. The name was an abridgment of the diminutive "Lepkeleh" ("Little Louis" in Yiddish) that his mother had called him as a boy. After his father died, his mother's health began to fail. The doctors recommended she move to Arizona to improve her health; Buchalter was left as his sister's responsibility. The day his mother boarded the bus to leave the city was the last time his sister ever saw him. At fifteen Lepke left school to work as a delivery boy.

By the time Lepke was eighteen, his whole family moved west. Lepke then moved to the Lower East Side where he started his criminal career. He joined a local gang that did petty crimes. This is when he got close to Jacob Gurrah Shapiro and they stayed close for over thirty years. After his nineteenth birthday Lepke was sent to jail for theft and was paroled in 1917.

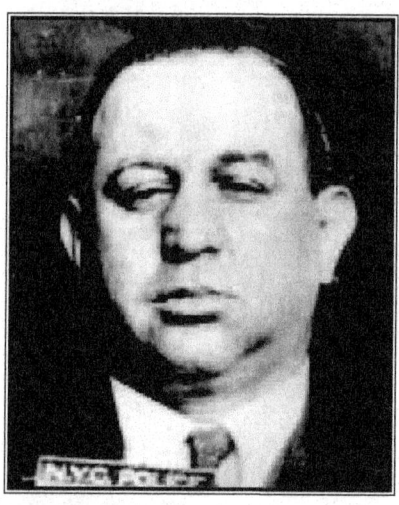

Jacob Gurrah Shapiro, a close friend to Lepke for over thirty years.

The following year he was back in on larceny charges, released, and then arrested again in 1920 on burglary charges and went to prison for two years. When he got out, lucky Lepke didn't get arrested until 1939. When he got out he turned to labor racketeering; the gang's method was violent. The unions had to pay Lepke protection from unionizers and strikers, or the crew terrorized them with beatings and murder. Sometime in the 1930's Lepke joined the national crime syndicate with Bugsy Siegel, Meyer Lansky, Dutch Schultz, Longy Zwillman, Lucky Luciano, Frank Costello and Joe Adonis. At Lepke's suggestion they created a crew to maintain order and contract killings. The original members were a Brooklyn based gang of Jewish hoods run by Abe "Kid Twist" Reles, Harry "Pittsburgh Phil" Strauss, Abraham "Pretty" Levine, Martin "Bugsy" Goldstein, together with the Italian crew lead by Harry "Happy" Maione and Frank "Dasher" Abbandando.

Lepke and his syndicate including Benjamin "Bugsy" Siegel.

| Dutch Schultz | Joe Adonis | Frank Costello | Abe "Kid Twist" Reles |

A crime reporter in the 1930's named Harry Feeney coined the name "Murder Inc". Brownsville covered 2.19 square miles but packed in over 200,000 people. It was the most densely populated community in the borough. Pitkin Avenue was packed with shops, food carts, and delis. The language heard in the street was predominately Yiddish. On the corner of Livonia Avenue, just up from the train station at 779 Saratoga Avenue sat Midnight Rose's candy store. The boys would meet up each day to think up scams, pick up assignments, or just sit around playing cards. The boys referred to themselves as the "Brownsville Troop" and at their peak numbered as many as thirty. The store was owned by a sixty year old immigrant named Rose Gold. The store was called Midnight Rose's, as she would leave the store open 24 hrs. for the boys. Rose and her son Sam Siegal helped Reles with his loan sharking operation, also with the help of her daughter Shirley Herman.

37 - Brooklyn Gangsters

Some of the crew Lepke had at hand at the store were Seymour "Blue Jaw" Magoon, Mendy Weiss, Vito "Chicken Head" Gurino, "Little Farvel" Cohen, Sholem Bernstein, Dukey Maffeatore and Alli "Tick Tock" Tannenbaum. Some worked independently and some worked in groups, but make no mistake, they were all killers..

Buchalter's downfall began in the mid-1930's, so he went on the lam to elude the Federal Bureau of Investigation, which wanted him on a narcotics charges. The New York authorities were also desperate to nail him for his "Murder, Inc." and "Syndicate" activities. There was a $50,000 reward out for Lepke, but for two years he remained free. He was hiding out right under their noses, for Lepke had never left Brooklyn. Moey Dimples, the Saratoga numbers man who had been a friend to Lepke since their days of strong-arming cart vendors, was one of the few people who Lepke still trusted and who knew where he was, so Lepke had little reason to doubt Dimples when he approached Lepke and told him.

Albert Anastasia told Lepke to turn himself in and that they would take of care of the charges, so Lepke left his Coney Island hideout and traveled over the Brooklyn Bridge through the Manhattan warehouse district to turn himself over to the F.B.I, but not to F.B.I. agent Dewey.

Federal Prosecutor Tom Dewey.

Rumor has it that Lepke surrendered to Walter Winchell. However, Anastasia reneged on the deal and Lepke was sentenced to fourteen years at Leavenworth State Penitentiary in Kansas for narcotics trafficking. The sentence was extended to thirty years for Lepke's union racketeering. Even more legal problems followed in 1940 when the state of New York indicted Lepke for a murder committed four years earlier. On September 13th, 1936, acting on Lepke's orders, "Murder, Inc." killers brutally murdered a Brooklyn businessman named Joseph Rosen.

Joseph Rosen, a Brooklyn businessman who was brutally murdered by killers in Murder Inc. on Lepke's order.

Rosen was a former garment industry trucker whose union Lepke took over in exchange for ownership of a Sutter Avenue candy store. Lepke told Rosen to leave town, and Rosen did, until the money ran out. Then he came back to the Brooklyn candy store. When Lepke got wind of it ,he went wild and wanted him to leave, but Lepke heard (with no proof) that Rosen was working with the district attorney's office, so Lepke put a hit on Rosen. Abe "Kid Twist" Reles overheard this information and turned state's evidence in 1940 and fingered Buchalter for four murders. Lepke returned from Leavenworth to Brooklyn to stand trial for the Rosen slaying. Buchalter's position was worsened by the testimony of Albert Tannenbaum. Four hours after they were handed the case, the jury arrived at a verdict, at 2 a.m. on 30 November 1941, finding Buchalter guilty of first degree murder, the penalty for which was death by electrocution. Also convicted and sentenced to death for the same crime were two of Buchalter's lieutenants who had participated in the planning and commission of the Rosen murder, Emanuel "Mendy" Weiss, and Louis Capone (no relation to Al Capone).

Buchalter's conviction took place in December 1941, and the New York Court of Appeals, on review of his case, upheld his conviction and death sentence in October 1942, by a vote of 4-3. (People v. Buchalter, 289 N. Y. 181). Two of the dissenting judges thought the evidence was so weak that errors in the judge's instructions to the jury as to how to evaluate certain testimony were harmful enough to require a re-trial. The third dissenter agreed, but added that, in his opinion, there was insufficient evidence to sustain a guilty verdict, so the indictment should be dismissed altogether (failure of proof means no retrial). The United States Supreme Court granted Buchalter's petition to review the case and in a full opinion affirmed the conviction, 7-0, with two justices abstaining. (319 U.S. 427 (1943)) In the Supreme Court, Buchalter was represented by Arthur Garfield Hays, a leader of the trial bar who was general counsel for the ACLU and had a private practice consisting of wealthy, powerful clients.

At the time of the affirmation of his conviction, Buchalter was serving his racketeering sentence at Leavenworth Federal Prison, and New York state authorities demanded he be turned over to them for execution. Buchalter resisted, managing to remain in Kansas and out of New York's hands until extradited in January 1944. Buchalter and his lieutenants, Weiss and Capone, were electrocuted within minutes of each other at New York's Sing Sing prison on 4 March 1944. No longer would there be a national enforcement arm of the "Syndicate". The mob had evolved into a more business-like enterprise, with less unification and more internal strife.

The electric chair at New York's Sing Sing Prison. Lepke and his lieutenants, Weiss and Capone, were electrocuted within minutes of each other.

There are those who would argue that this was always the case with organized crime, and who doubt the romantic notion of a stable of killers sitting around waiting for orders from a national board of directors. They say mobsters only killed when necessary for the course of business. That may be the case. But for a ten-year period after the ascension of Lucky Luciano, there did exist a small band of killers who reveled in their work, took pleasure in killing for business and who saw the gun as a means to further commerce. These were the killers of "Murder, Inc".

Somewhere between seventy-five and one hundred men were murdered on Lepke's order either shot, stabbed, iced picked, or burned to death. The Midnight Rose's crew had a lot of blood on their hands. It is even said that Lepke coined the phrase "hit", meaning a contract for a murder. We were told that they got the saying "those good old Jewish boys" from "The Brownville's Troop". I heard that saying for years not knowing what the hell they were talking about. After reading the articles about "Murder Inc", I now know what they meant.

Louis "Lepke" Buchalter walking with Federal Agents. It is said that Lepke coined the phrase "hit" meaning a contract for a murder.

The gravesite of Louis "Lepke" Buchalter. (Top)
A side and front shot of the sinister Louis Lepke. (Bottom)

41 - Brooklyn Gangsters

Grand Central Terminal often incorrectly called Grand Central Station, or shortened to simply Grand Central is a terminal station at 42nd Street and Park Avenue in Midtown Manhattan in New York City. Built by and named for the New York Central Railroad in the heyday of American long-distance passenger trains, it is the largest train station in the world.

Benjamin Siegel
February 28, 1906 - June 20, 1947

BENJAMIN SIEGEL
BUGSY

Siegel was born Benjamin Siegelbaum on February 28, 1906, in the Williamsburg section of Brooklyn. He was the second born of five children but was the only one to be drawn in by the criminal element that ruled the streets of Williamsburg. Brooklyn, in the early part of the 20th Century, was a melting pot of America. Within its tight confines lived thousands of Irish, Italian and Jewish immigrants, all struggling to make a life for themselves in the New World. The streets were lined with tenements, which were wrenched with poverty and disease. Pushcart vendors hawked their goods, yelling in Yiddish or Italian and ethnic tensions were always high in the neighborhood. As a youngster, Ben's best friend was Moey Sedway, a diminutive lackey who was willing to go along with whatever plans Ben was hatching. Their favorite pastime was when Ben would go up to a vendor and ask for a dollar. As the vendor told Ben to scram, Ben would have Moey splash the papers and magazines with kerosene and set them on fire. The next time the boys came around, the vendor was usually willing to pay up. From there, Ben and Moey moved into a protection scam, taking money from the vendors in the street in return for making sure no one else pulled the same scam against them. While Ben was running this protection racket, he met another immigrant teen outlaw with big plans, Meyer Lansky, the man who would shape his life, and eventually, his death. Lansky, who had already met a young Salvatore Luciano, later known as Lucky Luciano, saw that the Jewish boys of his Brooklyn neighborhood needed to organize in the same manner as the Italians and Irish. The first person he recruited for his gang was Ben Siegel. On January 28, 1929, Siegel married Esta Krakower, his childhood sweetheart and sister of hit man Whitey Krakower.

Meyer Lansky met Siegel when he was young and recruited him as part of his street gang.

Salvatore "Lucky" Luciano, an Italian who associated with Siegel and Lansky.

44 - Brooklyn Gangsters

Siegel and Meyer started out in auto theft and ended up handling hit contracts for bootleggers who were having their shipments hijacked. This tidy little killing business was the forerunner to the infamous "Murder Incorporated," which handled hundreds of contract murders during the 1930's.

Siegel and Meyer's gang mates included Abner "Longie" Zwillman, Lepke Buchalter, the future head of Murder Inc., and the only top mobster to get the chair, plus Lansky's brother, Jake and a young Arthur Flegenheimer, who would go on to make a name for himself as Dutch Schultz. They also became acquainted with many syndicate legends like Little Moe, Big Greenie, Willie Moretti, Joe Adonis and Kid Twist Reles. By the end of 1918, the Bugs and Meyer mob was in full swing, operating closely with Lucky Luciano and his right-hand man, Frank Costello. Although the Sicilians and the Jews were separate gangs, there was a bond between the two groups, something that was unusual at the time. Both Lansky and Luciano refused to be limited by the old rules that said Italians were Italians, Jews were Jews, and not to do business with each other. The Bugs and Meyer mob and Luciano's boys were busy terrorizing the people of New York. Pawnbrokers, moneylenders and immigrant businesses were most often their shakedown or robbery targets. Meanwhile, the gang began to use its bankroll to buy into established bookmaking operations and to buy the protection of the police and politicians who ran the Lower East Side.

For the first time, the Bugs and Meyer mob came to the attention of the real powers in New York City, Joe "The Boss" Masseria and Arnold Rothstein. The welcomes they got from the two men were decidedly different. Masseria had decided to bring the Lower East Side under his control and the Bugs and Meyer mob was standing in the way. Masseria was an old-time gangster who was never interested in cooperation with non-Sicilians.

Arnold "The Brain" Rothstein- a high-stakes gambler in New York during the time Bugsy and Lansky were up and coming.

On the orders of Joe "The Boss" Masseria in early 1919, a crap game that was operating under the protection of Meyer was raided by a group of men who proceeded to beat up the game's organizers, bodyguards and customers. The hoods told Lansky that this was a warning: unless tribute was paid, killings would follow. Meyer and Bugs weren't ready to cave in. They hunted down the Italians who led the raid when the men told them that Joe "The Boss" would make them pay for their insolence with their lives. They backed off and regrouped. It didn't matter to Bugsy that Masseria had a 200-man army and that the Bugs and Meyer mob was at best a couple dozen strong. Now was the time to go on the offensive.

Siegel and several other Turks from his gang returned to Masseria's boys and this time they didn't back down. A huge fight ensued and the Masseria boys were routed. By the time the battle was over, the cops arrived and Lansky, Siegel and some of his hoods were arrested. The charge was disorderly conduct and carried a two-dollar fine.

Misdemeanor charges aside, the fight sent a clear message to Masseria, one he took to heart — the Lower East Side and Brooklyn belonged to the Bugs and Meyer mob. Masseria also wanted Luciano to sever his ties with the Bugs and Meyer mob, something Charlie would not do. With the enactment of the Volstead Act in 1919, the manufacture and sale of alcohol became illegal in the United States. For gangsters like Bugsy Siegel, this was a license to steal across the country. Speakeasies, blind pigs and bathtub gin joints sprang up with amazing frequency. Bootleggers smuggled booze across every border, in trucks, boats and pipelines. Judges were reluctant to enforce the penalties of the Volstead Act and police would often be paid off to look away. Prohibition did little to curb the consumption of alcohol and only served to provide the underworld with access to easy money in the billions. Rothstein, a.k.a. "The Brain", was mostly a high-stakes gambler who knew a good thing when he saw it. Rothstein wanted to make money during Prohibition, but he wanted to do it high class. To do this, he needed partners. He turned to Charlie Luciano and the Bugs and Meyer mob.

Summoned to Rothstein's Central Park residence, Meyer Lansky and Charlie Luciano were offered their chance at the big time. Rothstein proposed that under the direction of the Bugs and Meyer mob — specifically Lansky (he had no patience for a man of Bugs' temperament) — Dutch Schultz would take over the New York bootlegging operation and Longy Zwillman, Lansky's close Friend, would run North Jersey. Other men who were later brought into the operation included the dapper Guiseppe Doto, a.k.a. Joe Adonis, Carlo Gambino (the future head of the Gambino crime family), Vito Genovese, Gambino's predecessor as godfather, and the sinister Albert Anastasia.

As cover for their rum running operation, Siegel and Lansky operated a car and truck rental operation through a garage on Cannon Street in Brooklyn. Ironically, Lansky's skill as a businessman made the rental business almost as much of a success as the bootlegging. Bugsy was the point man for the rum running racket. Lansky was never shy about lending a hand when an extra gun was needed, but it was Siegel who craved the excitement of taking a shipment of illegal booze or highjacking another gang's property. Lansky and Siegel were still anxious for revenge for Masseria's attempted power grab in Brooklyn. Bugsy found out when Masseria's load of booze was going to the boss of Philadelphia, Waxy Gordon. He traveled down to Atlantic City NJ and set up an ambush where they knew Masseria's boys would be coming. They placed a tree on the road and then hid in the nearby woods, waiting for the truck convoy to approach. Thanks to a two-grand bribe, Siegel knew exactly when and where the shipment would be coming. As soon as the group approached the tree, a hail of bullets rained down on them and sent them scrambling for cover. A furious gun battle ensued, and three of Masseria's men fell. As the battle turned in favor of Siegel and his men, they emerged from the woods and began clubbing and beating the remaining Italians who had surrendered. In the course of this savagery, one of Masseria's men recognized Meyer Lansky. Waxey Gordon learned that the Bug and Meyer mob was responsible for his loss, but because he didn't want Rothstein to know he was working with Masseria, Rothstien's Sicilian adversary, he kept his mouth shut. But Gordon didn't forget, and like Masseria, who was still courting Luciano, he vowed to get revenge. Rothstein had forbidden his crew from stealing from one another and the penalty for such insolence would probably be death. Bug and Meyer survived the next decade and made millions in bootlegging during Prohibition. By the end of the Roaring 20's, Masseria had succeeded in convincing Charlie Luciano to join his team. Charlie continued to interact with Siegel and Lansky, but he was consumed by a war between the Masseria and Maranzano factions. For nearly two years, the gangs waged war on each other. The attrition was eating up both sides, but it soon became clear to Siegel and Lansky that Maranzano was willing to work with them. Sal had been lobbying for Luciano's loyalties and even though Lucky was working for Masseria, Maranzano still wanted his help. The men of the Bugs and Meyer mob met with Luciano and hatched a plan.

Accompanied by Ben Siegel, Luciano met with Maranzano on the neutral turf of the Bronx Zoo. There, Luciano agreed to join Maranzano's gang. He would be Maranzano's lieutenant and he would maintain his own operations with the Jewish gangsters as well as share in the Sicilian's spoils. His initiation fee would be Joe Masseria's life. Luciano invited his boss to Villa Tammaro Restaurant in Coney Island on April 15, 1931. The two men enjoyed a fine meal of the house specialties and fine Italian red wine. After more than three hours of feasting, Luciano excused himself to use the bathroom. As Masseria sat at the table where he and his loyal lieutenant had been planning the eradication once and for all of the Maranzano gang, a crew of gunmen rushed in and shot him to death.

Leading the charge was Benny Siegel, guns blazing. Six bullets found Joe the Boss who was desperately trying to find a place to hide. Fourteen more slugs sprayed into the wall behind him.

With Joe either dead or dying, the four gunmen, Siegel, Vito Genovese, Albert Anastasia and Joe Adonis, rushed from Villa Tammaro into the waiting car with the driver, Ciro Terranova. The four gunmen escaped before the police arrived and found the boss of bosses dead. Soon after, Lucky Luciano had Joe Maranzano assassinated, and he had his opening to start his National Crime Syndicate. In 1932, Siegel was arrested for gambling and bootlegging but got off with a fine. Lansky and Siegel assisted in Luciano's brief alliance with Dutch Schultz and killed rival loan shark Louis "Pretty" Amberg and Joseph Amberg in 1935. In 1937, the East Coast mob sent Siegel to California to develop syndicate gambling rackets with Los Angeles mobster Jack Dragna. Once in Los Angeles, Siegel recruited gang boss Mickey Cohen as his lieutenant. Siegel used syndicate money to set up a national wire service to help the East Coast mob quicken their returns.

"Bugsy" Siegel next to his car around the time of the Maranzano murder which Siegel performed with the help of notorius gangsters Vito Genovese, Joe Adonis and Albert Anastasia.

Siegel moved Esta and their two daughters, Millicent and Barbara, to California. On tax returns he claimed to earn his living through legal gambling at Santa Anita Park near Los Angeles.

On November 22, 1939, Siegel, Whitey Krakower, and two other gang members killed Harry "Big Greenie" Greenberg. Greenberg had become a police informant, and Louis "Lepke" Buchalter, boss of Murder Inc, ordered his killing. Siegel was tried for the Greenberg murder. Whitey Krakower was killed before he could face trial. Siegel was acquitted but his reputation was in ruins. During the trial, newspapers revealed Siegel's past and referred to him as "Bugsy". He hated the nickname (said to be based on the slang "bugs", meaning "crazy", and used to describe his erratic behavior), and wouldn't be called "Bugsy" to his face.

Siegel had traveled to Southern Nevada in 1934 with Meyer Lansky's lieutenant Moe Sedway on Lansky's orders to explore expanding operations. There were opportunities in providing illicit services to the crews constructing the Hoover Dam. Lansky had turned the desert over to Siegel. Siegel, wanting nothing to do with it, turned it over to Moe Sedway and fled for Hollywood.

Lansky pressured Siegel to represent them in Wilkerson's desert project, The Flamingo Hotel. Siegel proved useful to watchdog their interests. Siegel, who knew Wilkerson and lived near him in Beverly Hills, was the obvious choice as a liaison, but Siegel was infuriated. He wanted no part in any operation that took him back to Nevada permanently. It meant forsaking Beverly Hills and playboy life and enduring the heat of Nevada. At Lansky's insistence, however, Siegel consented. Throughout the spring of 1946, Siegel proved useful.

Then problems came when Siegel demanded more involvement in the project. To keep the project moving, Wilkerson agreed that Siegel would supervise the hotel while Wilkerson retained control of everything else.

In May 1946, Siegel decided the agreement had to be altered to give him control of the Flamingo. Siegel offered to buy out Wilkerson's creative participation with corporate stock - an additional 5 percent ownership in the operation. On June 20, 1946, Siegel formed the Nevada Project Corporation of California, naming himself President. He was also the largest principal stockholder in the operation, which defined everyone else merely as shareholders. From this point the Flamingo became syndicate-run.

The Flamingo Hotel and Casino in Las Vegas Nevada, which was controlled by Siegel for only one year before the operation shut down in 1947.

The first indication of trouble came in early November 1946. The syndicate issued an ultimatum: provide accounting or forfeit funding. But producing a balance sheet was the last thing Siegel wanted to do. After the syndicate's refusal of help, Siegel waged a campaign of private fund raising; he sold nonexistent stock. Siegel was in a hurry to finish. He doubled his work force, believing the project could be completed in half the time. But it was costs, not building, that began rising faster. Siegel paid overtime and double-time. In some cases, bonuses tied to project deadlines were offered in hope of increasing productivity. By the end of November, work was nearly finished and the opening had been set for December 26th 1946.

While locals jammed the opening, few celebrities materialized. A handful did motor in from Los Angeles despite appalling weather. Some of the celebrities present were June Haver, Vivian Blaine, George Raft, Sonny Tufts, Brian Donlevy and Charles Coburn. They were welcomed by construction noise and a lobby draped with decorators' drop cloths. The desert's first air conditioning collapsed regularly. While gambling tables were operating, the luxury rooms that would have served as the lure for them to stay and gamble longer were not ready. After two weeks the Flamingo's gaming tables were $275,000 in the red and the entire operation shut down in late January 1947. By begging the mob bosses to give his friend a second chance, Lansky got an extension for Bugsy. After being granted a second chance, Bugsy cracked down and did everything possible to turn the Flamingo into a success. However, by the time profits began improving, the mob bosses above Bugsy were tired of waiting.

Benjamin "Bugsy" Siegel with Hollywood actor George Raft.

On the night of June 20, 1947, as Siegel sat with his associate Allen Smiley in Virginia Hill's Beverly Hills home reading the Los Angeles Times, an unknown assailant fired at him through the window with a .30-caliber military M1 carbine, hitting him many times, including twice in the head. No one was charged with the murder, and the crime remains officially unsolved.

Though descriptions held that Siegel was shot in the eye, he was actually struck twice on the right side of his head. Both death scene and postmortem photographs clearly show that one shot penetrated his right cheek and exited through the left side of his neck; the other struck the right bridge of his nose where it met the right eye socket. Overpressure created by that bullet's striking and passing through Siegel's skull blew his left eye out of its socket. Both the Los Angeles' Coroner's Report (#37448) and his death certificate (Registrar's #816192) state the cause of death was cerebral hemorrhage.

Though as noted, Siegel was actually not shot exactly through the eye (the eyeball would have been destroyed if this had been the case), the bullet-through-the-eye style of killing nevertheless became popular in Mafia lore and in movies, and was called the "Moe Greene special" after the character Moe Greene - based on Siegel - who was killed in this manner in The Godfather.

Siegel was hit by several other bullets including shots through his lungs, According to Florabel Muir, "four of the nine shots fired that night destroyed a white marble statue of Bacchus on a grand piano, and then lodged in the far wall. That was the end of the Bug and Meyer gang. Bugsy died just like he killed...violently.

Virginia Hill, Bugsy's girlfriend. It was in her home, where Bugsy was slain.

Siegel, dead after 2 bullets to the head. One was rumored to have been shot through his eye, becoming the inspiration for "The Moe Greene Special" from the movie *The Godfather*.

50 - Brooklyn Gangsters

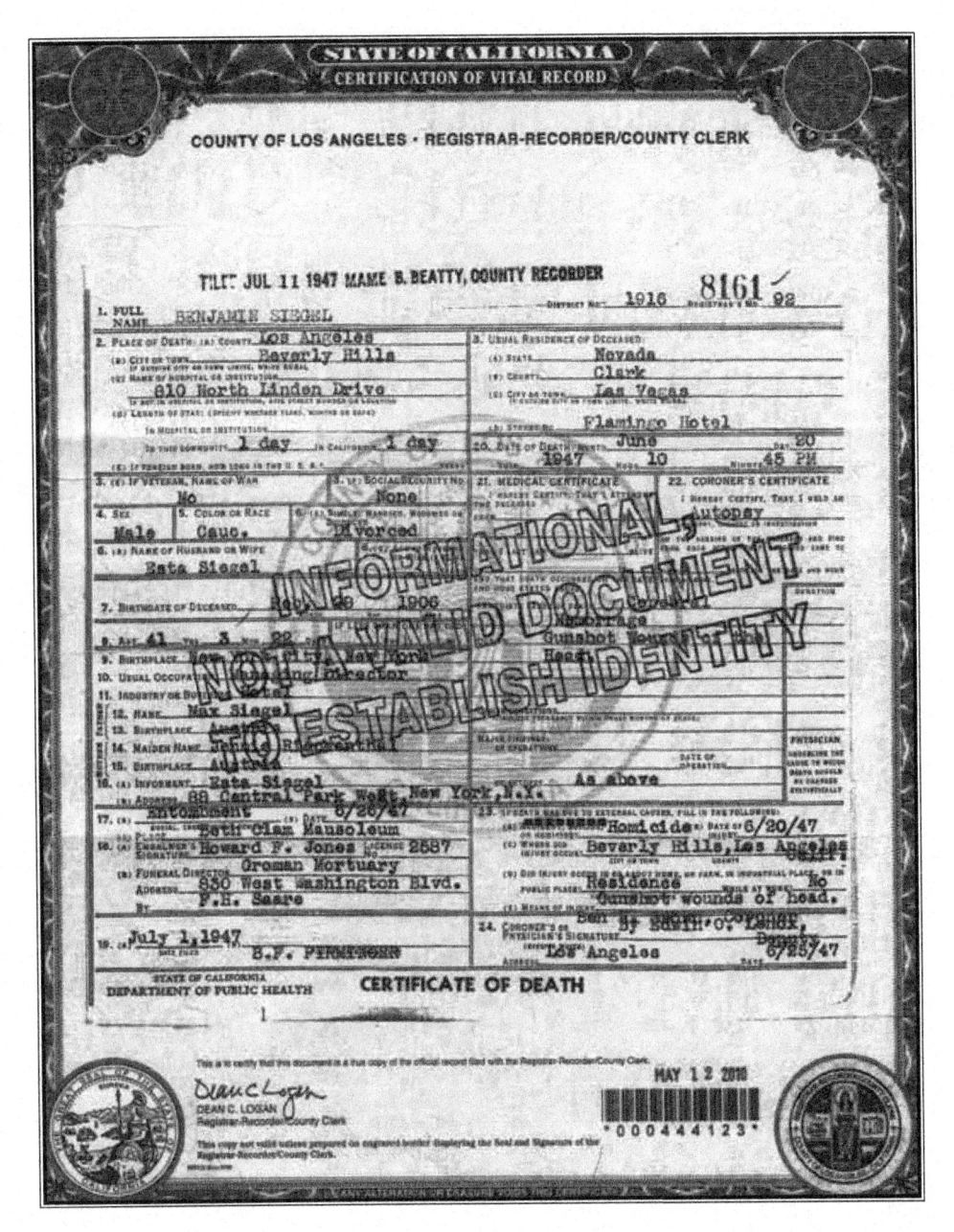

The death certificate of Benjamin "Bugsy" Siegel. Siegel was hit by several other bullets including shots through his lungs According to Florabel Muir, "Four of the nine shots fired that night destroyed a white marble statue of Bacchus on a grand piano, and then lodged in the far wall. That was the end of the Bug and Meyer gang. Bugsy died just like he killed...violently.

This plaque still stands at the site of the famous "Flamingo Hotel and Casino". The plaque describes the grand "Bugsy Suite" or the "Presidential Suite" as it was sometimes called, which only had one entrace, but several convinient exits. It is now owned and operated by the Hilton Hotel chain.

52 - Brooklyn Gangsters

The Brooklyn Historic Railway Association's shop, trolley barn and offices are located in Red Hook, Brooklyn, New York, on the historic Beard Street Piers (circa 1870). Brooklyn's first trolley car run on Coney Island Avenue in 1890 ran in Brooklyn until the late 1950's.

53 - Brooklyn Gangsters

Albert Anastasia
September 26, 1902 - October 25, 1957

ALBERT ANASTASIA
LORD HIGH EXECUTIONER

Albert Anastasia born Umberto Anastasio, September 26, 1902 - October 25, 1957, was born in Tropea, Calabria, Italy and was one of nine brothers. Anastasia moved to New York City with his family around 1919; he was 17. His parents Raffaelo Anastasia (1869-1920) and Louisa Nomina de Filippi (1885-1925) also gave birth to three other boys, Anthony Anastasia (1906-1963), who was also involved in crime, Gerardo Anastasia and Salvatore Anastasia (1919-1973). The family eventually relocated to Union St. in the Red Hook section of Brooklyn. He became active in Brooklyn's waterfront operations and rose to a position of authority in the longshoremen's union, the ILA located on Court Street in Red Hook, Brooklyn. It was here that Anastasia first demonstrated his penchant for homicide at the slightest provocation, killing a fellow longshoreman in the early 1920s – an offense which led to an 18-month sentence at Sing Sing Prison in Ossining, New York. He met some gangsters in jail who liked his toughness. They arranged in the street to kill all the witnesses in his case. By doing this, Albert received a new trial and had his conviction overturned. Back on the streets, Albert spent a lot of time in Red Hook with a small crew of young Turks. From the docks, to the local bars, from Columbia St. to Court St. he would rule like a madman. Albert had a seat at a bar called Hanley's Saloon on 3rd place and Court St.

The longshoremen's union, the ILA located on Court Street in Red Hook, Brooklyn. It was here that Anastasia first demonstrated his penchant for homicide.

55 - Brooklyn Gangsters

Hanley's Saloon where Albert spent a lot of time. He even had his own stool that was only brought out when Albert came in.

If anyone would go near it he would go into such a rage that the owner would put the bar stool in the back until he got there. Early in his organized crime career, Anastasia served in a gang led by Giuseppe "Joe the Boss" Masseria. Anastasia was always a devoted follower of others, primarily Charles "Lucky" Luciano, Frank Costello and Jimmy "The Shiv" Destefano. His loyalty during the Castellammarese War was to the boss of what is now called the Gambino Crime Family, one of New York City's "Five Families." From 1951-1957 he also ran a gang of contract killers called Murder Inc. which enforced the decisions of the Commission, the ruling council of the American Mafia. He was nicknamed the "Mad Hatter" and the "Lord High Executioner". He was added to this esteemed group due to his own reputation as a cold-blooded killer. He was one of the most intimidating figures in organized crime at that time. Mobsters who'd racked up a number of notches on their own belts reported chills going through their bodies when they sat across a table from him for some dispute or other. A cigarette usually dangled almost vertically downward from his lips, making him squint icily; his huge hands appeared as though they could rip a man apart in seconds. A sudden move by Albert at the sit-down would have made them shutter in fear.

Giuseppe "Joe the Boss" Masseria

Charles "Lucky" Luciano

Frank Costello

56 - Brooklyn Gangsters

In 1930, Luciano finalized his plans to take over the organized crime rackets in New York by destroying the two old Mafia factions headed by Masseria and Salvatore Maranzano. Luciano outlined his plot to Anastasia, who joined him and Benjamin "Bugsy" Siegel in the plot. Anastasia assured Luciano that he would kill everyone for him to reach the top. Anastasia knew that if Luciano ran the National Crime Syndicate, he would eventually get a "piece of the action." Anastasia was a member in the four-man group that gunned down Masseria in Nuova Villa Tammaro, a Coney Island restaurant, on April 15,1931.

He also became one of the founding members of the modern day criminal organization that was born at the 1931 gathering in Atlantic City. The meeting, which was hosted by Luciano, included mob figures from around the country, including Meyer Lansky, Frank Costello, and Al Capone.

To reward Anastasia's loyalty, Luciano placed him and Louis "Lepke" Buchalter, the nation's leading labor racketeer, in control of the Syndicate's enforcement arm, Murder, Inc.. The crew, also known as "The Boys from Brooklyn," was a group of mainly Jewish killers that operated out of the back room of Midnight Rose's, a candy store in the Brownsville neighborhood of Brooklyn. During its ten years of operation, it is estimated that Murder, Inc. committed between 200 and 400 murders, many of which were never solved. Unlike Lepke and many other members of Murder, Inc., Anastasia was never prosecuted for any of these murders since, as the underboss of a family, he had his own killers to use if needed. During this period, Anastasia's business card claimed that he was a "sales representative" for the Convertible Mattress Corporation in Brooklyn.

Murder, Inc. maintained its power until the early 1940's. After his arrest, hit man Abe "Kid Twist" Reles made a deal granting him immunity from prosecution. Reles' testimony helped convict many of the group's hit men, including co-boss Buchalter. In retaliation, Anastasia promised a $100,000 reward for Reles' death.

In 1936, US Attorney Thomas Dewey convicted Luciano on a pandering charge. Luciano received a 30 to 50 year sentence. During World War II, Anastasia reportedly originated the plan to win a pardon for Luciano by helping the war effort.

Benjamin "Bugsy" Siegel

Nuova Villa Tammaro, where Albert shot down Joe Masseria in 1931.

57 - Brooklyn Gangsters

With America needing allies in Sicily to advance the invasion of Italy, and the desire of the Navy to dedicate its resources to the war, Anastasia orchestrated a deal to obtain lighter treatment for Luciano while he was in prison, and after the war, a parole in exchange for the Mafia protecting the waterfront and Luciano's assistance with his associates in Sicily.

Despite being a mob power in his own right, Anastasia was nominally the under boss of the Mangano crime family. Through the years, boss Vincent Mangano had fumed at Anastasia's closeness to Luciano, Costello, and others. Mangano was particularly irked that Luciano and Costello obtained Anastasia's services without first seeking Mangano's permission. This and other business disputes almost led to blows between Mangano and Anastasia, and it was only a matter of time before one or the other was ordered killed. In early 1951, Vincent Mangano went missing, and his brother Phil was murdered. Although Vincent Mangano's body was never found, it is widely presumed that he and his brother were murdered by Anastasia.

Abe "Kid Twist" Reles, the turncoat who helped bring down many of the top hit men in Murder, Inc.

Boss Vincent Mangano, who went missing in 1951, presumed to have been murdered by Anastasia.

After the deaths of the Mangano brothers, Anastasia claimed that they were trying to kill him and claimed control of the family with Costello's active support. With this much clout, the Commission confirmed Anastasia's ascension. He also gained the support of Mangano's old friend, Joe Bonanno, who grew close to Anastasia.

As long as Costello (and before him, Luciano) were in control, they were able to hold Anastasia's violent instincts in check. However, as a crime boss, Anastasia, if possible, turned even more violent than before. For instance, when he saw Arnold Schuster informing on the whereabouts of Willie Sutton, Anastasia flew into a rage. "I can't stand squealers!" he screamed. "Hit that guy!" Schuster was gunned down a few days later.

Arnold Schuster, the upstanding citizen who'd done what he felt was his duty, was shot twice in the groin and once in each eye even though it was in no way connected to mob business.

Vito Genovese cunningly used Anastasia's brutal behavior against him in an effort to get Anastasia's supporters away. Secretly over the next few years, Genovese won the cooperation of Anastasia's under boss, Carlo Gambino. However, Genovese dared not move against Anastasia and his real target, Costello, because of Meyer Lansky, an influential and rich mob associate. Lansky and Genovese were long-standing enemies, with disputes dating from the 1920's. Genovese could not make a power play without Lansky's support.

Anastasia's ambition soon drove Lansky to help Genovese. During the 1950's, Lansky was extremely successful in controlling casino gambling in Cuba, offering other Mafia bosses lesser shares of his profits and interests. When Anastasia forcefully demanded a larger piece of the action, Lansky refused. Anastasia then started establishing his own gambling racket in Cuba. Lansky became increasingly angry with Anastasia, and while Lansky preferred watching Anastasia and Genovese battle each other from the sidelines, he now gave active support to Genovese's plan to kill Anastasia.

Willie Sutton

Meyer Goldstein, a Murder, Inc. associate.

The opportunity came to light when it became known that Anastasia had been selling memberships in his family, charging fifty thousand dollars a pop to bestow "dunsky" status. This term was what "made guys" were commonly called in those days, for those who could afford it. Anastasia's long lasting legacy was that his successor, Carlo Gambino, closed the "books" to new members being admitted in order to clean house of the unfit wise-guys Albert had anointed for cash. Other than a small number of exceptions, that ban stayed in effect until Gambino's death in 1978.

On the morning of October 25, 1957, 55 year old Anastasia entered the barbershop of the Park Sheraton Hotel (now the Park Central Hotel, on 56th Street and 7th Avenue) in Midtown Manhattan. Anastasia's bodyguard parked the car in an underground garage and then took a walk. As Anastasia relaxed in the barber chair, two men, scarves covering their faces, rushed in, shoved the barber out of the way, and fired at Anastasia. After the first volley of bullets, Anastasia allegedly lunged at his killers. However, the stunned Anastasia had actually attacked the gunmen's reflections in the wall mirror of the barbershop. The gunmen continued firing and Albert Anastasia finally fell to the floor, dead. The Anastasia murder remains officially unsolved. It is widely believed that the contract was given to Joe Profaci, who passed it on to "Crazy Joe" Gallo from Brooklyn, who then performed the hit with one of his brothers. At the same time Profaci was an ally of Joe Bonnano who, together with Anastasia, formed a three family foil to the ambitions of Genovese/Costello and Luchesse. By killing Anastasia, Profaci would have been eliminating an ally in favor of a new potential enemy in Gambino who had even stronger ties to Luchesse.

"Crazy Joe" Gallo, a infamous mob hitman from Brooklyn.

The barbershop of the Park Sheraton Hotel (now the Park Central Hotel, on 56th Street and 7th Avenue) in Midtown Manhattan where Anastasia was shot.

At the time of the murder, Joe Bonanno had been attending a meeting in Sicily with Lucky Luciano and other major organized crime figures. Bonanno had been seen as a close ally of Anastasia and many felt the timing of the hit had to do with his absence.

After his assassination, the barber chairs at the Park Sheraton Hotel were turned around to face away from the mirror.

Anastasia was buried in Green-Wood Cemetery in Brooklyn, New York, in Section 39, Lot 38325.

Nathan's began as a nickel hot dog stand in Coney Island in 1916 and bears the name of co-founder Nathan Handwerker. The original Nathan's still exists on the same site that it did in 1916. Everyone you can think of ate a hotdog there, from Al Capone to the last president. Surf and Stillwell Avenues at Coney Island.

Giuseppe Carlo Bonanno
January 18, 1905 – May 11, 2002

JOSEPH CHARLES BONANNO
JOE BANANAS

Bonanno was born Giuseppe Carlo Bonanno on January 18, 1905 in Castellammare del Golfo, a town on the western coast of Sicily. He was an only child. Bonanno was married to Fay Labruzzo. They had three children: Salvatore "Bill" Bonanno, born in 1932, Catherine, born in 1934, and Joseph Charles Jr., born in 1945.

His mother Catherine Bonvente was the sister of Stefano Magaddino, a Mafia boss in Sicily. His father Salvatore was the leader of the Bonanno clan in Sicily, the leading family of the Castellammare, a man of honor. His father had to leave Sicily to avoid prosecution. Joe was three years old when his family moved to the United States and settled in Williamsburg, a neighborhood in South Brooklyn, at North Fifth Street and Roebling. The neighborhood was a mix of Jews, Poles, Armenians, and Germans.

The cops and politicians were all Irish and treated everyone like animals if they weren't Irish. You see foreigners had this crazy idea that America was this land of opportunity and freedom, but they didn't know it was run by a bunch of prejudiced gangs that ran the city. From the street gangs to the law, they had a hatred for the Italians. They even liked the blacks better. That really blows my mind because from what I heard, they hated them too. When the family got here, Salvatore opened a pasta store downstairs from their apartment and across the street he opened a tavern to serve his paisans. After ten years in America, the Bonannos had to go back to Italy. The family needed Salvatore because there was trouble in the family. After settling the family matters, Salvatore got drafted into the Army and died shortly after getting wounded in World War I. Joe continued his education in Sicily, eventually going to Joeni Trabia Nautical Institute in Palermo. After three years of being there, Mussolini started the Fascist Movement. Joe did not want to be involved in it so he quit school and went back home to Sicily at the age of nineteen. He could not stay in Sicily any longer so he headed back to America in 1924. Back in America, Joe got involved with the Castellammarese faction. Here they knew his father was a man of honor, so Joe moved right in and started his life in crime. From the beginning, Bonanno was recognized by New York and Brooklyn "Mafia families" as a man with pedigree. They knew of his family in Sicily and his knowledge of the organization. He caught the eye of one of the leaders of a "Mafia family" in New York, Joe "the Boss" Masseria. Masseria became increasingly suspicious of the growing number of Castellammarese in Brooklyn. He sensed they were separating themselves from his

A leader of a Mafia family in New York, Joe "The Boss" Masseria.

64 - Brooklyn Gangsters

overall leadership. A war broke out between Masseria and Maranzano, which became known as the Castellammarese War. It continued for more than four years. By 1930, Maranzano's chief aides were Bonanno as underboss, Tommy Lucchese and Joseph Magliocco. Tommy Gagliano ran another gang that supported Maranzano. The Buffalo, New York mob boss was Stefano Magaddino, and his son was Peter Magaddino. Peter was a boyhood friend of Bonanno from his student days in Palermo. Masseria had Lucky Luciano, Vito Genovese, Joe Adonis, Carlo Gambino, Albert Anastasia and Frank Costello on his side.

Tommy Lucchese

Joseph Magliocco

Albert Anastasia

Tommy Gagliano

Vito Genovese

Carlo Gambino

Frank Costello

Joe Adonis

Lucky Luciano

A third faction on the rise, composed of younger "Mafioso" on both sides were disgusted with the old world ideas of Masseria, Maranzano and other old-line Mafioso, whom they called "Mustache Petes." The new crew of "Young Turks" was led by Luciano and included Costello, Genovese, Adonis, Gambino and Anastasia. Although Bonanno came from "old-school" traditions of "honor," "respect" and "dignity" like others of his generation, he saw the need to modernize and joined forces with the Young Turks.

By 1931, momentum had shifted to Maranzano and the Castellammarese faction. They were more well organized and more unified than Masseria's men, some of whom began to defect. Luciano and Genovese urged Masseria to make peace with Maranzano, but Masseria stubbornly refused. In the end, Luciano and Genovese planned a hit on Masseria with Maranzano, in return for safety and to be a "capo" in Maranzano's new organization. Luciano and Genovese murdered Masseria and ended the Castellammarese War.

After Masseria's death, Luciano outlined a peace plan to all the Sicilian and Italian gang leaders in the United States. Under his plan there would be five families throughout the United States who would elect their own bosses. In New York City, five Mafia families were established, headed by Luciano, Profaci, Gagliano, Vincent Mangano and Maranzano. At the head of the whole organization would be the "capo di tutti capi" (the boss of bosses). Maranzano thought he was the one. This was not in the plans of Luciano or the rest of the new crews. As a consequence, Luciano arranged Maranzano's murder.

Bonanno was given most of Maranzano's crime family. At age 26, Bonanno became one of the youngest ever bosses of a crime family. Years later, Bonanno wrote in his autobiography that he didn't know about the plan to kill Maranzano (bullshit). They all got together and planned the hit on the "Mustache Petes." How I know this, is one of Bonanno's lawyers is an uncle of mine and out of Joe's mouth he said that "if he didn't go with Lucky he was dead too, case closed".

In place of the capo di tutti capi, the new plan was that Luciano would establish a National Commission in which each of the families would be represented by their boss. Each family would run their designated area, but the Commission would arbitrate disputes between gangs. The purpose of this organization was to prevent another bloodletting like the Castellammarese War, and according to Bonanno, it succeeded. The establishment of the Commission ushered in more than 20 years of relative "peace" to the New York and national organized crime scene. Bonanno wrote: "For nearly a thirty-year period after the Castellammarese War it worked."

The Bonanno crime family's underbosses were Frank Garofalo and John Bonventre. While it was traditionally one of the smaller of the five New York families, it was more tightly knit than the others. With almost no internal dissension and little harassment from other gangs or the law, the Bonanno family prospered in the running of its loan sharking, bookmaking, numbers running, prostitution, and other illegal activities. Let's not forget murder.

Bonanno made a ton of money in the syndicate, allowing him to make many profitable real estate investments during the Great Depression. His legitimate business interests included the garment industry, cheese factories, funeral homes, and a trucking company. Joe Bonanno owned a funeral parlor in Brooklyn, which was utilized as a convenient front for disposing of bodies. The funeral home's "clients" were provided with double-decker coffins, and more than one body would be buried at once. This method was used right up until a few years ago. The New Jersey Delcavalcante family was doing it till a "rat" blew it. Unlike most of the Mafioso of the time, Bonanno lived the lavish lifestyle. He associated with most gangsters of his time. He preferred meeting with his "soldati" in his Brooklyn home. The only encounter Bonanno had with the law during these years was when a clothing factory that he partly owned was charged with violating the federal minimum wage per hour law, and the company was fined $50. Bonanno was only a shareholder in the company and was not fined. Government officials later arrested Bonanno, claiming he had lied on his citizenship application by concealing a criminal conviction; the charge was dismissed in court. Despite this, Bonanno was all but unknown to the general public until the disastrous Appalachian Conference of 1957. He was one of the few bosses not to be arrested. However, not long afterward, a federal grand jury began a major investigation into organized crime, and prosecutors identified him as the leader of a major crime family. He was indicted for obstruction of justice after refusing to testify before the grand jury, but suffered a heart attack before the trial. After numerous postponements, the United States Court of Appeals threw out the indictment.

After the death of Joe Profaci, a very good friend of Bonanno, and leader of the Profaci crime family, Profaci was succeeded by another good friend of Bonanno's, Joe Magliocco. Soon, Magliocco began to have troubles with the rebellious Joe Gallo and his brothers Larry and Albert, who were now backed by Lucchese and Gambino. Meanwhile, Bonanno was also feeling threatened by Lucchese and Gambino. The two then planned to have Gambino and Lucchese killed, as well as Bonanno's cousin Magaddino and Frank DeSimone in Los Angeles. Magliocco gave the contract to one of his top hit men, Joseph Colombo. However, Colombo betrayed his boss and went instead to Gambino and Lucchese. Gambino called an emergency meeting of the Commission. They quickly realized that Magliocco could not have planned this by himself. Remembering how close Magliocco (and before him, Profaci) had been with Bonanno, it didn't take them long to conclude that Bonanno was the real mastermind.

At Gambino's suggestion, the Commission ordered Magliocco and Bonanno to appear for questioning. Bonanno didn't show up, but Magliocco did and confessed. In light of Magliocco's failing health, the Commission imposed a very lenient punishment—a $50,000 fine and ordering him to hand over leadership of his family to Colombo. Soon, Magliocco was dead from high blood pressure. They intended to let Bonanno off easily as well, wanting to avoid a repetition of the bloodbaths of the 1930's.

After several months with no response from Bonanno, they removed him from power and replaced him with one of his capos, Gaspar DiGregorio. Bonanno, however, would not accept this. This resulted in his family breaking into two groups, the one led by DiGregorio, and the other headed by Bonanno and his son, Salvatore. Newspapers referred to this as "The Banana Split."

A young Joe Bonanno.

Since Bonanno refused to give up his position, the other Commission members felt it was time for drastic action. In October 1964, Bonanno was allegedly kidnapped by Buffalo family members Peter Magaddino and Antonio Magaddino. According to Bonanno, he was held captive in upstate New York by his cousin, Stefano Magaddino. Supposedly Magaddino represented the Commission, and told his cousin that he "took up too much space in the air", a Sicilian proverb for arrogance. After much talk, Bonanno was released. The Commission members believed he would finally retire and relinquish his power.

Bonanno's hold on his family had become weak. Many family members complained that Bonanno was almost never in New York and spent most of his time at his second home in Tucson, Arizona. However, Bonanno was unwilling to accept the Commission's edict, and rallied several members of his family behind him. The family split into two factions, the DiGregorio supporters and the Bonanno loyalists. The Bonanno loyalists were led by Bonanno, his brother-in-law Frank Labruzzo and Bonanno's son Bill. There was no violence from either side until a 1966 Brooklyn "sit-down." DiGregorio's men arrived at the meeting, and when Bill Bonanno arrived, a large gun battle ensued. The DiGregorio's loyalists planned to wipe out the opposition but they failed and no one was killed. Further peace offers from both sides were spurned with the ongoing violence and murders. The Commission grew tired of the affair and replaced DiGregorio with Paul Sciacca, but the fighting carried on regardless.

The war was finally brought to a close with Joe Bonanno, still in hiding, suffering a heart attack and announcing his permanent retirement in 1968.

Bonanno and his son Bill subsequently moved to Arizona, where he was at one time sent to jail by the Federal Bureau of Investigation to serve time for various offenses during his previous stay in that state. In 1983, he wrote his autobiography *A Man of Honor*. The government seized the opportunity and questioned him about the Commission, hoping to prove its existence given that he spoke about it in his book. Technically, he kept the vow of "omertà" and answered no questions in government hearings, but many then-current New York Mafia leaders were outraged at what he had said in his book and considered him to have already broken the vow. Despite an arrest record dating back to the 1920's, Bonanno was never convicted of a serious crime. He was once fined $450 and held in contempt of court for refusing to testify in 1985. Assigned federal inmate number 07255-008, he was transferred from the Federal Correctional Institution in Tucson, Arizona to the U.S. Medical Center for Federal Prisoners in Springfield, Missouri due to ill health at his advanced age and released on November 1, 1986. Upon retirement, he was allowed to live in peace at his home in the Blenman-Elm neighborhood of Tucson, Arizona with his family.

Bonanno, the last remaining "Mafia Don" who survived Italian fascism, Mustache Petes, and his own bloody war, died on May 11, 2002 of heart failure at the age of 97. He is buried at Holy Hope Cemetery & Mausoleum in Tucson.

Bonanno is said to have been one of the models for the character "Vito Corleone" in Mario Puzo's novel, "The Godfather."

Joe Bonanno's gravesite in Tucson, Arizona.

Pin Boys, this is how they used to do it. The game took a little longer but nobody worried about time and most kids made a few cents a day. Some gangsters started that way but now they are all gone.

Paul Vario
July 9, 1914 - November 22, 1988

PAUL VARIO
BIG PAULIE

The Vario family originated from Sicily. The etymology of the Vario surname is that it was originally a nickname given to a person who lives in or comes from the property of Vannius. Paul Vario was born in the East New York section of Brooklyn, just before the roaring twenties. He was one of five brothers.

Paulie's brothers were Vito 'Tuddy' (1928–1988), Salvatore (1919–1976), Leonard (1909–1981), and Thomas Vario (1917–1984). He was also a relative of Boston, Massachusetts' Whitey Bulger, and associate Benedetto "Chubby" Oddo (1939-). Like himself, most of his brothers would also participate in criminal activities as part of the Lucchese family. Paul Vario was a maternal cousin of Colombo crime family consigliere John "Johnny O" Oddo and his brother, "mobster" Steven "Little Stevie" Oddo.

Paul had three sons with his first wife, and then divorced and married a woman named Phylis. His sons were named Peter "Petey" Vario, Paul "Little Paulie" Vario Jr., and Leonard "Lenny" Vario, all of whom became involved in crime. Lenny was allegedly Paul Sr.'s favorite son who had burned to death while torching property in connection with a union. Little is known about his other son, Peter.

Vario was the grandfather of actor Paul Vario who appeared in the mob thriller "This Thing of Ours," with James Caan, Frank Vincent, and Vincent Pastore. He first got involved with the mob during the mid 1920's, quickly developing a reputation as a ruthless leader who would take down anyone betraying him without hesitation. He was involved in a massive variety of crimes, including murder, robbery, illegal gambling, and selling stolen goods. The federal prosecutors that put him in prison said it all by calling him "one of the most violent and dangerous career criminals in the city of New York".

Vario listed his legal career as a florist, but next to that, he was mostly involved in policy gambling, loan sharking, extortion and burglary. His first convictions go back to 1931. He was arrested for many crimes, ranging from tax evasion to rape. During the 1950's Vario headed a crew of Lucchese gangsters, said to have been the "strong-arm faction" of the family.

Vario and his crew also maintained influence at Kennedy International Airport, extorting shippers and airlines in exchange for labor peace. They also frequently stole from the airport's cargo center. During the 1950's Vario became associated with an Irish gangster named Jimmy Burke. Burke specialized in burglary and was known for his violent nature. Other well known members of Vario's crew were Henry Hill and Tommy DeSimone. Both were also made famous in the movie "Goodfellas" and frequently worked together with Burke.

Kennedy International Airport.

Henry "the Rat" Hill

Tommy DeSimone

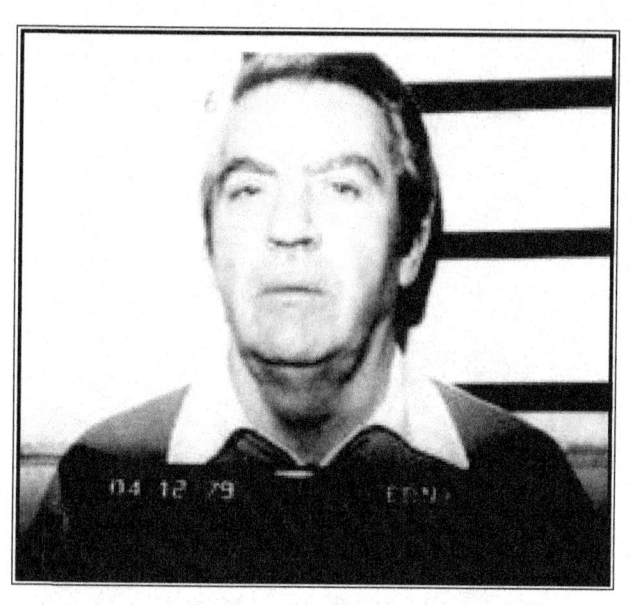

Jimmie Burke, who specialized in violence and whom Vario associated with.

Paulie was very good at keeping the other families from going to war with his "outfit." He had a diplomatic skill that allowed him to run his businesses without too much trouble and to settle differences before they erupted into war. His diplomatic skills also assisted him in union corruption operations, where his crew extorted millions of dollars every year from businesses that did not want union strikes to cause them to lose their place in the market. When things got too hot, witnesses disappeared and people with outstanding loans received "encouragement".

He and his brothers were involved in a number of legitimate businesses, including a flower shop, restaurant, and cabstand, from which he would conduct business most of the time. Brother Vito "Tuddy" Vario ran the "Euclid Avenue Cab Company" and "Presto Pizzeria". At his highest point, Vario was earning an estimated $25,000 a day. Vario and his brothers, along with their criminal associates, operated in the Brownsville section of Brooklyn, in East New York. Both the cabstand and pizzeria were located in close proximity, on Euclid Avenue and were popular hangouts for the crew. Vario was one of the richest leaders of the crime families in the 50's. In the late 60's "Paulie" Vario became a "capo" in the Lucchese family.

Paul, or "Paulie" as his friends called him, was known for his size. He was about six feet tall and weighed close to 250 pounds over the majority of his life. His appearance resembled that of a sumo wrestler, with jowls hanging below his chin, likening his appearance to that of a ferocious bulldog. He moved slowly through life because he felt that he didn't have to move quickly for anyone and figured things would bend to his will, one way or another. His speaking often consisted of short "grunt-like" responses.

Vario never used a private telephone because he always believed it was too easy for someone else to overhear his conversations. Instead he would meet with his soldiers or other intermediaries who would talk to the people that Vario needed to communicate with. Paulie was well known for his paranoia. He was very careful about putting his name on things. He only used public pay phones on the street. Even his boat he docked in Sheepshead Bay had no name. He didn't like to speak out loud in public about dealings, instead always whispering.

Although Vario reputedly treated Henry Hill like a son, he also had an affair with his wife Karen during the late 1970's. At one point, Tommy DeSimone tried to rape Karen. Vario was furious and took measures. He went to see members of the "Gambino Family" and revealed to them that DeSimone was responsible for the murder of 2 of their men, one being William Devino, a made member. DeSimone was protected throughout the years, but now it came to an end. In 1979 DeSimone was lured to a house with the false pretense of finally being "made" inside the Lucchese Family, but instead he was shot through the head by Tommy Agro, a Gambino member.

In 1972 the FBI had placed a "bug" in the Vario headquarters for about 6 months, and as a result, Vario and a couple of others, including Henry Hill, were arrested. They were imprisoned in Lewisburg and, according to Hill, they lived there like kings. They were placed in a large cell and had all sorts of privileges, including having their own cook. Hill was even permitted to deal drugs while in prison. He was, however, told by Vario to stop his involvement in the drug business from the moment he was out of jail. After that it would be nothing but convictions and trials for Vario.

In April 1973 he was sentenced to 6 years and fined $20,000 for income tax evasion. In 1980 Henry Hill became a federal witness out of fear of getting murdered from the orders of Burke and Vario. Hill had continued his drug dealing without permission and also had knowledge of the Lufthansa Heist, which was organized by Burke, and was one of the largest robberies ever in America.

Paul Vario's Junkyard in New York.

Burke had gone on a killing spree after the heist, and Hill got scared that he was going to be next. Due to Hill's testimonies, Vario was found guilty in 1984 for defrauding the government by helping Hill get out of prison several years earlier. He had helped Hill in getting a job in a restaurant to win his release from prison. A couple of years later, Vario and 4 others pleaded guilty of extorting $1 million from trucking companies at Kennedy International Airport. On December 10, 1986, he was sentenced to 6 years and was fined another $25.000. By then Vario was suffering from bad health and eventually died in 1988 of lung failure in Fort Worth Federal prison, Texas, at the age of 73. He left behind his wife and 3 sons.

I met "Big Paulie" in the 1970's. My father helped him with some trouble he was having with some shipping company at Kennedy airport that wanted to unionize. My father had the connections to either stop it or help it go though. He had a deal with Joe Schipini who was with Lucky Luciano. Uncle Joe was getting old but he still had the unions by the balls, so for a couple of weeks, we ate with Paulie at the "Skyway" hotel near the airport. He was, to say it nicely, a rough looking guy but he was a great host. My father made a long term friendship with him and I became the liaison between them. He always treated me with respect so I have "nuttin" to say bad about him. Yes he was a little intimidating, but we were dealing with killers. At the end my father did a few years in prison with Paulie, not on the same charges. I guess all gangsters eventually meet in jail. Paulie died there and my father came home.

76 - Brooklyn Gangsters

Stickball, a game played in the streets from the turn of the century until now. Whether you were black or white, it didn't matter when you played ball.

Roy Albert DeMeo
September 7, 1942 – January 10, 1983

ROY DeMEO
THE BUTCHER

Roy Albert DeMeo was born in 1942 in Bath Beach, Brooklyn into a working class Italian immigrant family. DeMeo graduated from James Madison High School in 1959 and began working in criminal enterprise while maintaining legitimate business practices. He married shortly after high school and fathered three children. As a teen, he began a small loan sharking operation, which turned into a full time job by the age of 17. Not coming from money, he looked for ways to make money from hanging out with the sons of a neighbor, Mafia boss Joseph Profaci. Roy learned about loan sharking: someone with means loaned money to people who could not get loans from regular venues, such as banks, and for this favor, they would then charge exorbitant interest rates. At first, Roy's assignments were just to pick up the interest owed each week from various businesses, but eventually he learned how to make the loans on his own. He was drawn more deeply into organized crime and was exposed to the ways of the southern Italians who had been transplanted to New York.

Gambino soldier Anthony Gaggi took notice of DeMeo and told him that he could make even more money with his successful business if he came to work directly for the Gambino family. DeMeo's organized crime prospects increased on two fronts. He continued in the loan sharking business with Gaggi, and began developing a crew of young men involved in car theft and drug trafficking. It was this collective of criminals that would become known both in the underworld and in law enforcement circles.

Gambino soldier Anthony Gaggi who took notice of DeMeo and told him that he could make even more money with his successful business if he came to work directly for the Gambino family.

By the early 1960's DeMeo had quit his legitimate job at a Banner Dairy Supermarket to focus on loan sharking and any other opportunities for income. He conducted most of his business at a neighborhood bar, Phil's Lounge. In 1965, he became a silent partner of the bar, now renamed the Gemini Lounge, located at Flatlands Avenue and Troy Avenue in the heart of Brooklyn. The Lounge served as the DeMeo crew's headquarters for the next several years, with apartments above and behind. The bar was the site of dozens of murders and dismemberments committed by the crew.

The Gemini Lounge located at Flatlands Avenue and Troy Avenue
in the heart of Brooklyn.

Anthony Senter    **Chris Rosenberg**    **Joey Testa**    **Henry Borelli**

Roy was 32, living in a nice home in an exclusive community with his wife and children, when he committed his first murder for the family. He was running an extortion scheme with Anthony against a lucrative X-rated film business, when the owner and his partner were arrested. It appeared that one of them, Paul Rothenburg, might offer up his association with Roy and Nino in a deal. Roy scheduled a meeting with him at a diner, to assist with legal expenses. When they got out of their cars, Roy pulled a pistol with a silencer, took the businessman into an alley, and shot him in the head seven times. Now that he had killed, it was just business as usual to him. In fact, he was known to say, "once you've killed someone, you can do anything".

Thereafter, he began to train a crew of young men to become killers and to get rid of a body quickly and efficiently. Roy had once been a butcher's apprentice, so he understood how to cut limbs from bodies. Among DeMeo's initial recruits was a 16-year-old Jewish kid named Chris Rosenberg, who despised his ethnicity and desperately hoped he could one day prove himself so the Italians would welcome him as one of their own. Roy met Chris in the Brooklyn neighborhood of Canarsie, where Chris was dealing pot, and helped him to move into a larger money-making arena. He got Chris and his friends into the business of stealing cars that could be turned into saleable items for wealthy clients overseas. A car mechanic named Freddy DiNome joined them, then two more friends, high school dropouts, Joey Testa and Anthony Senter. Joey and Anthony hung out at the Gemini Lounge so often they were dubbed "The Gemini Twins". A fifth young man with a killer's cold heart, Henry Borelli, came onto the team and they would all meet at this bar to socialize and organize their illegal business operations. Roy began collecting weapons and he kept his impressive arsenal of machine guns, automatic rifles, and silencers in a room at the lounge. He put his cousin, whose nickname was "Dracula," into one of the apartments to watch over his stash.

Roy devised a specific form of getting rid of someone, which eventually came to be known as "The Gemini Method". He trained his crew how to participate in a "dis-assembly" line. If someone needed to be "made a memory," disposal was always a problem, so his method appeared to be an answer.

The target person, whom someone higher up had ordered eliminated, would be invited into DeMeo's Gemini Lounge. He'd be shot at once by one crew member (often Roy himself), wrapped in a towel by another to prevent blood from messing the place up, and repeatedly stabbed in the heart by yet a third person to quickly decrease blood flow. Then he'd be cleaned up and allowed to "settle" for 45 minutes by hanging upside down over a bathtub in Dracula's apartment. Drained of blood, laid out on a swimming pool liner, beheaded, and hacked into pieces, the various parts were then packaged in plastic garbage bags and tossed into a dump. "Just like taking apart a deer", DeMeo told his gang; there was no real difference.

However, this manner of disposal had to be refined. The first time they tried it, on a criminal car dealer who'd turned informant in 1975, they were careless. First Chris, Joey and Anthony used a pretty girl to lure Andrei Katz, so she was a witness. Next, they hauled him off the streets publicly, leaving his car open and empty—clearly a missing person. Then they took him into the supermarket where they met Roy. There he told them the plan and they had to go with it or their lives would on the line. It was the moment of truth for all of them—could they deal with hacking a human being apart?

On this day Chris used a butcher knife to still the man's heart by piercing it clean through several times. Then he repeatedly stabbed him in the back. The crew wore butcher aprons to proceed. In an act of overkill, Chris ran Katz's head through a compacting machine, and the others wrapped the body parts in bags. Then they dumped these packages into a garbage bin to be hauled away. However, the team had miscalculated when the garbage collection would occur, giving a homeless man ample time to pull open the packages and expose the human body parts. He ran, but another man coming along saw what it was and called the police. In all, they found eight neatly wrapped packages but never did find the genitals. The coroner who examined the mess and eventually identified the remains was Roy's second cousin.

The girl who had innocently lured the doomed victim read about his death in the papers and turned on the crew. The police arrested two of them, but no evidence connected them to Roy. He got them a lawyer, but they had to serve some time. When their trial came, their lawyer undermined the girl's credibility and the two crew members were acquitted.

Roy devised a specific form of getting rid of someone, which eventually came to be known as "The Gemini Method". He trained his crew how to participate in a "dis-assembly" line.

After that, the crew took on the added chore of taking the parts themselves to the dump. A few were buried beneath ongoing construction, and one was sealed into a barrel into which concrete was poured, but it appeared that the standard disposal was the local garbage dump.

Such "disappearances" happened frequently and systematically—by some estimates, in less than a decade there were between seventy-five and two hundred. The five men involved in the dis-assembly line said to associates that they got a kick out of it. They used to say "killing made them feel like God".

Richard Leonard "The Iceman" Kuklinski was an American mobster and contract killer. The six foot five, 300 pound Kuklinski worked for Newark's DeCavalcante crime family and New York City's Five Families. He claimed to have committed his first murder at the age of 13 and claimed to have murdered over 250 men between 1948 and 1986.

Richard Kuklinski's association with the Gambino crime family came through his relationship with the capo regime Roy DeMeo, which started due to a debt Kuklinski owed to a DeMeo crew member. DeMeo was sent to 'talk' with Kuklinski and proceeded to beat him with a pistol. Although Richard was carrying a pistol at the time, he decided against pulling it out. This earned him DeMeo's respect.

After Kuklinski paid back the money he owed, he began working for DeMeo and the Gambino family, one of which was pirating pornographic tapes.

According to Kuklinski, one day DeMeo took him out in his car and they parked on a city street. DeMeo then selected a random target, a man walking his dog. He then ordered Kuklinski to kill him. Without hesitating, Kuklinski got out, walked towards the man and shot him in the back of the head as he passed by. From then on, Kuklinski was DeMeo's favorite enforcer.

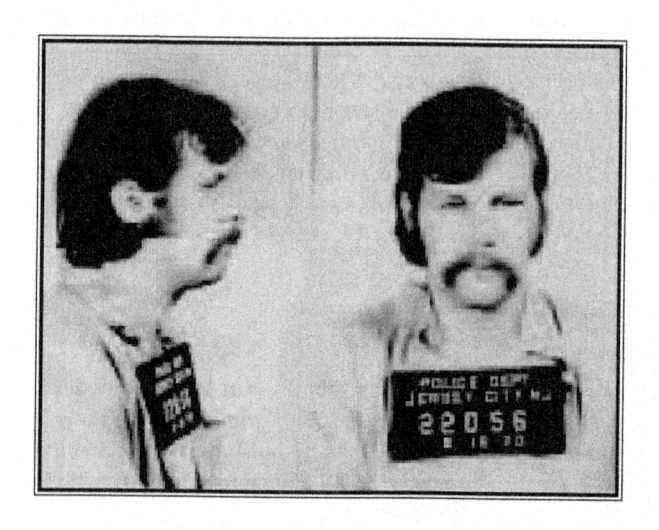

Richard Leonard "The Iceman" Kuklinski, DeMeo's favorite enforcer. He worked for Newark's DeCavalvante family and New York's Five Families as a contract killer. He claimed to have committed his first murder at the age of 13.

In late 1979, DeMeo and Anthony Gaggi became involved in a conflict with James Eppolito and James Eppolito Jr., two made Gambino members in Gaggi's crew. They were both respectively the paternal uncle and cousin of the corrupt former New York City Police Department detective, Louis Eppolito.

Eppolito met with Paul Castellano and accused DeMeo and Gaggi of drug dealing, which carried the penalty of death. Castellano, to whom Gaggi was a close ally, sided against Eppolito in the situation and gave Gaggi permission to do what he pleased. He and DeMeo shot the two to death in Eppolito Jr's car en route to the Gemini Lounge on October 1, 1979. A witness who was driving by right as the shots were fired alerted a nearby police officer who arrested Gaggi after a shootout between the two that left Gaggi with a bullet wound in his neck.

Because DeMeo had split up with Gaggi after the shooting, he was not arrested or identified by the witness. Gaggi would be charged with murder and the attempted murder of a police officer, but through jury tampering, was convicted only of assault and given a 5 to 15 year sentence in Federal Prison. DeMeo would murder the witness shortly after Gaggi's sentencing in March 1980.

By 1982, the FBI was investigating the a number of missing and murdered persons who were linked to DeMeo or who had last been seen entering the Gemini Lounge. It is around this time that an FBI bug in the home of Gambino family soldier Angelo Ruggiero picked up a conversation between Angelo and Gene Gotti, John Gotti's brother.

In the conversation, it was discussed that Paul Castellano put out a hit on DeMeo, but was having difficulty finding someone willing to do the job. Gene Gotti mentioned that his brother John was wary of taking the contract, as DeMeo had an "army of killers" around him. It was also mentioned in this same secretly recorded conversation that, at that time, John had only killed 10 people, while DeMeo had killed at least 38. According to mob turncoat Sammy Gravano, eventually the contract was given to Frank DeCicco, but Frank and his crew couldn't get to DeMeo. DeCicco allegedly handed the job to DeMeo's own men.

Roy's son Albert DeMeo wrote that in his final days, DeMeo was paranoid and knew that he would be killed soon. DeMeo considered faking his own death and planned leaving the country. Instead, he left the house one day and never returned. Albert DeMeo later found DeMeo's personal belongings such as his watch, wallet, and ring in his study room.

On January 10, 1983, DeMeo went to crew member Patrick Testa's bodyshop for a meeting with his men. A few days later, on January 18, he was found murdered in his abandoned car's trunk. He had been shot multiple times in the head and had a bullet wound in his hand, from throwing his hand up to his face in a self-defense reflex when the shots were fired at him. Anthony Gaggi was suspected by law enforcement officials of being the one who personally killed DeMeo, although it is likely that crew members Joseph Testa and Anthony Senter were present as well.

Gaggi was not charged with the crime, although he was charged with a number of other murders. He died of a heart attack during his trial in 1988 at the age of 62. According to Anthony Casso's 2008 biography, DeMeo was killed at Patrick Testa's East Flatbush home by Joseph Testa and Anthony Senter following an agreement with Casso, who was given the contract by Gotti and DeCicco after they were unable to kill DeMeo during the fall of 1982. Casso said that DeMeo was seated, about to have a cup of coffee, when Testa and Senter opened fire. Anthony Gaggi was not present.

In April 1984, Colombo crime family soldier Ralph Scopo was overheard explaining to an associate that DeMeo had been killed by his own family because he was attracting too much attention from the FBI.

DeMeo's crew was soon rounded up. Henry Borelli, Joseph Testa, and Anthony Senter were imprisoned for life after two trials that saw them convicted of a collective total of 25 murders, in addition to extortion, car theft and drug trafficking. The convictions were secured in large part by testimony of former members Frederick DiNome and Dominick Montiglio. Paul Castellano was indicted for ordering the murder of DeMeo, as well as a host of other crimes, but was killed in December 1985 while out on bail in the middle of the first trial. The murder was ordered by John Gotti, who then became the new boss of the Gambino family.

Richard Kuklinski, a convicted contract killer, filled several contracts for DeMeo, and also claimed that he was the one who murdered him. He claims he shot him five times (twice in the head), and pistol-whipped his corpse, leaving him in the trunk of his car to be found. Just another story told by The Iceman!

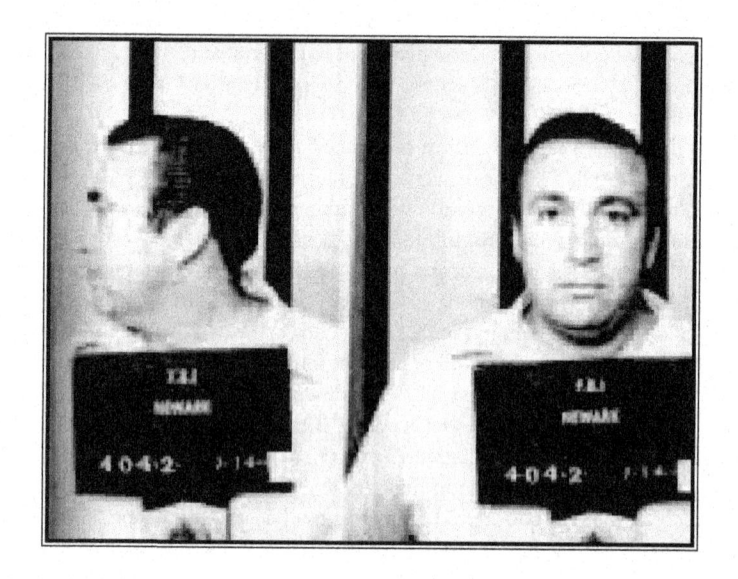

DeMeo considered faking his own death and leaving the country. However, instead he left the house one day and never returned. A few days later, on January 18, he was found murdered in his abandoned car's trunk. He had been shot multiple times in the head and had a bullet wound in his hand from throwing his hand up to his face in a self-defense reflex when the shots were fired at him.

Staubitz Market, established in 1917 by John Staubitz, originally opened as a butcher store, is one of the oldest food establishments still operating in Brooklyn. It has been in the McFadden family for over 40 years. John McFadden and his son, John McFadden, Jr. run it daily. It is located at 222 Court Street, Brooklyn.

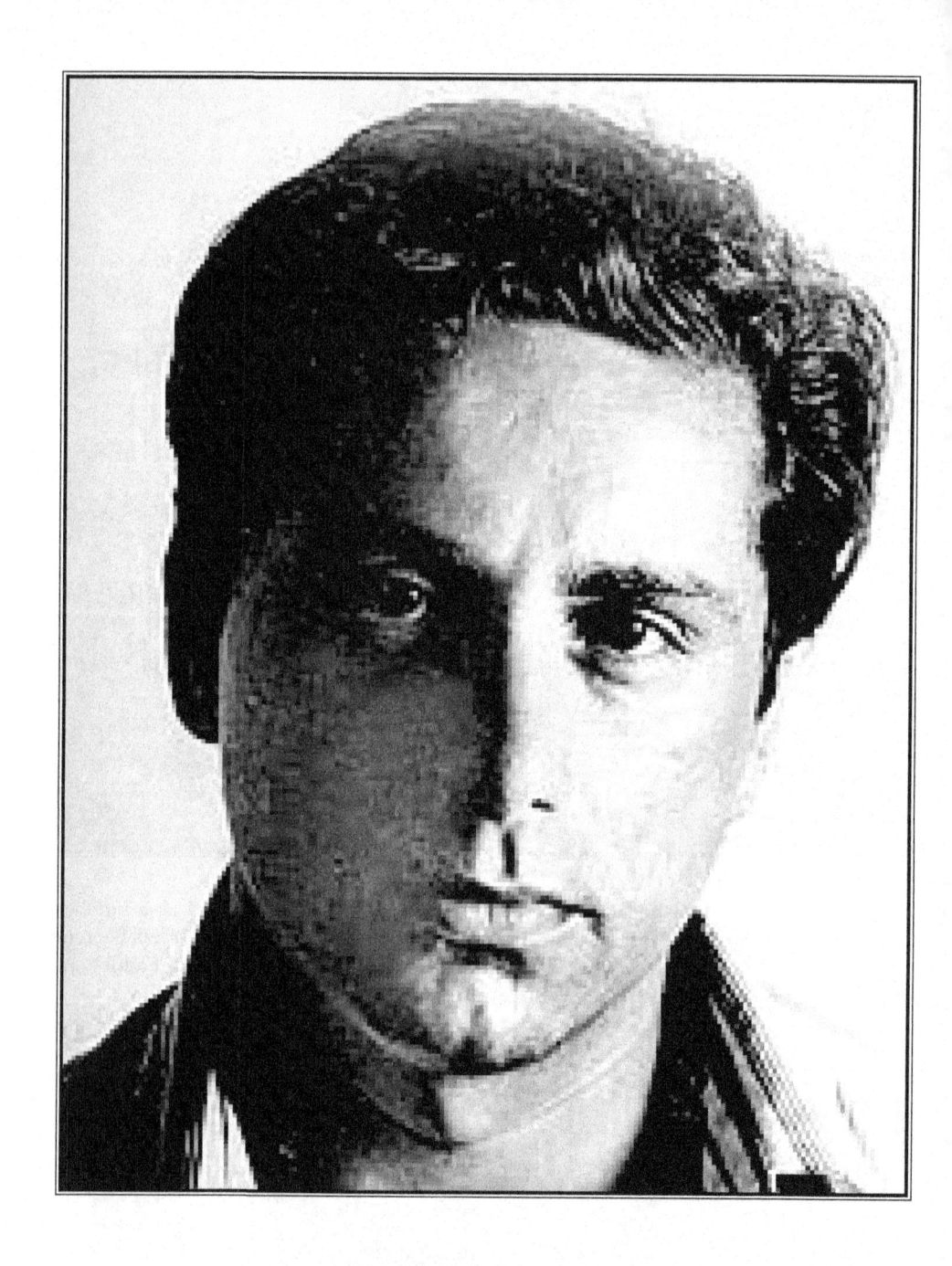

Anthony Casso
May 21, 1940 - Present

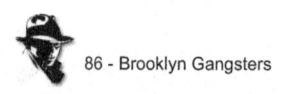

ANTHONY CASSO
GASSPIPE

Anthony "Gaspipe" Casso (May 21, 1940) was the youngest of the three children of Michael and Margaret Casso (née Cucceullo). Each of Casso's grandparents had imigrated from Campania, Italy, during the 1890's. Anthony was born in Park Slope, Brooklyn at Methodist Hospital on May 21, 1940. He had an older brother, Michael, and an older sister Lucille. Anthony's parents met at a bakery on Union Street and Bond Street that Margaret's parents owned in 1934 and married soon after. His godfather was Salvatore "Sally" Callinbrano, a "Capo" in the Genovese crime family who maintained a powerful influence on the Brooklyn docks. He made sure Anthony's father always had a job on the docks. Anthony had a view of "the life" from the inside through his godfather Sally. He took Anthony and his family on outings with some of his friends like Albert Anastasia, Joe Profaci and the Vito Genovese family. Even when he was back on the block where he lived at 719 Union Street, the neighborhood was filled with gangsters. Albert Anastasia had a club on Fifth Avenue and Carroll Street that Anthony's father would take him to as a young boy. Anthony became infatuated with guns and used to shoot from the rooftop with his friends, where he became very good with a gun. Anthony also made money shooting predatory hawks for pigeon tenders. When Anthony graduated from Francis Xavier Catholic Elementary School, his godfather gave him $50 cash. After his confirmation from St Francis Church on Carroll Street his godfather gave him a pinky ring, which started Anthony's love for jewelry.

Michael and Margaret Casso, imigrants from Campania, Italy who moved to America during the 1890's.

Sally Callinbrano's club where Anthony was first introduced to La Cosa Nosta.

Anthony was going to Manual High School on Seventh Avenue but had no interest in finishing, so he dropped out. He went to work at the docks with his father, with the help of his godfather Sally forging his birth certificate. He was a violent youth and a member of the infamous 1950's gang, the "South Brooklyn Boys." Anthony got his first pinch at an early age, the result of a gang war with the Irish. Casso soon caught the eye of Lucchese "Capo" Christopher "Christie Tick" Furnari. Casso started his career with the "Cosa Nostra" as a loan shark. As a protege of Furnari, Casso was also involved in gambling and drug dealing. The Lucchese crew started calling Casso "Gaspipe" when referring to him as a nickname. His father was known as "Gaspipe," a mob enforcer who used a gas pipe to threaten union dissidents and other victims. Even though Anthony detested the nickname, it stuck to him for life and though few would say it to his face, he allowed some close friends to call him "Gas".

Anthony "Gaspipe" Casso, who got his nickname from the Lucchese crew, the same nickname as his father.

88 - Brooklyn Gangsters

Christopher "Christie Tick" Furnari, the Lucchese capo who discovered Casso and brought him into La Cosa Nostra.

In the early 1960's Anthony shot a junkie that was harassing a woman in the neighborhood. The word went out in the "Cosa Nostra" that Anthony was ready to take his place in the "life". In 1968, Anthony would marry Lillian Delduca, a girl he knew from childhood. They had a daughter Jolene in 1971, and son Anthony, in 1974. They would move from Park Slope to Bensonhurst for a couple of years. Then Anthony thought it would be better to move to Mill Basin, a well to do neighborhood where a ton of wiseguys lived and which was also was closer to his business.

In the 70's Casso murdered a drug dealer on the orders of the boss of the Lucchese crew. The dealer was suspected of cooperating with the government. When Anthony was asked to do a favor, he did, no questions asked. In 1974 at age 32, Casso became a "made man" with the Lucchese family. Casso was assigned to Vincent "Vinnie Beans" Foceri's crew, who operated from 116th Street in Manhattan and from the "19th Hole," a lounge on Fourteenth Avenue in Brooklyn. In the 1980's Christie Tick made Anthony a "capo" of his own crew, but he turned it down, so he gave it to Vic Amuso.

Vic Amuso, the man who became capo of Christie Tick's crew after Casso turned down the role.

89 - Brooklyn Gangsters

Casso and Vittorio "Vic" Amuso started a partnership that would last for years. They committed scores of crimes, including drug trafficking, burglary and murder. When Furnari became the Lucchese consigliere, Casso's influence also increased.

Under the new Lucchese leader Amuso, Casso became the family underboss replacing Mariano Macaluso, who retired in 1989, although he wielded as much influence as Amuso. During this time, Casso maintained a glamorous lifestyle, wearing expensive clothes and jewelry (including a diamond ring worth $500,000), running restaurant tabs up to thousands of dollars, and owning a mansion in an exclusive Brooklyn area. While at the top of the Lucchese family, Amuso and Casso shared huge profits from their family's illegal activities. They received $245,000 annually from a major concrete supplier, the "Quadrozzi Concrete Company." Amuso and Casso also split more than $200,000 per year from the garment district rackets, as well as a cut of all the crimes committed by the family's soldiers.

Anthony "Gaspipe" Casso maintained a glamorous lifestyle, wearing expensive clothes and jewelry (including a diamond ring worth $500,000), running restaurant tabs up to thousands of dollars, and owning a mansion in an exclusive Brooklyn area.

Casso also controlled Greek-American gangster George Kalikatas, who gave Casso $683,000 in 1990 to operate a loan sharking and gambling operation in Astoria, Queens.

Casso also had a close alliance with Ukrainian mob boss Marat Balagula, who operated a multi-billion dollar gasoline bootlegging scam in Brighton Beach. Balagula, a Soviet Jewish refugee from Odessa, had arrived in the United States under the "Jackson-Vanik Amendment." After Colombo captain Michael Franzese began shaking down his underlings, Balagula approached Lucchese consigliere Christopher Furnari and asked for help. In response, the Lucchese family received a percentage of Balagula's gasoline profits. The money was strategically shared with New York's other four Mafia families and became the "Five Families'" biggest moneymaker after narcotics trafficking.

A blurry surveillence photo of Casso and Amuso.

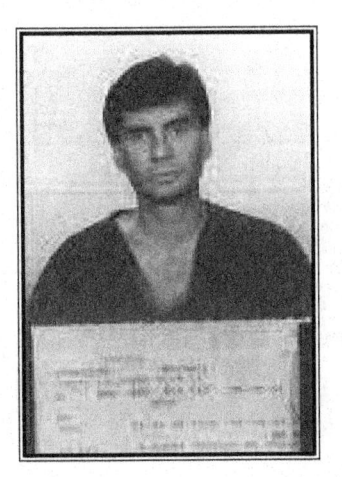

Colombo Captain Michael Franzese.

Shortly afterward, on June 12, 1986, Balagula's rival, a psychopathic hitman named Vladimir Reznikov, entered the "Rasputin" nightclub in Brighton Beach. Reznikov pushed a "9 mm Beretta" into Balagula's skull and demanded $600,000, the price of not pulling the trigger. He also demanded a percentage of everything Balagula was involved in. After Balagula promised to get the money, Reznikov snarled, "Fuck with me and you're dead -- you and your whole fucking family; I swear I'll fuckin kill your wife as you watch -- you understand?"

Shortly after Reznikov left, Balagula suffered a massive heart attack. He insisted, however on being treated at his home in Brighton Beach, where he felt it would be harder for Reznikov to kill him. When Anthony Casso arrived, he told Balagula, "Send word to Vladimir that you have his money, that he should come to the club tomorrow; we'll take care of the rest." Casso also requested a photograph of Reznikov and a description of his car.

The following day, Reznikov arrived at Balagula's nightclub to pick up his money. Instead, Reznikov was confronted by Gambino associate Joseph Testa, who fatally shot him on Casso's orders. According to Casso, after that, Balagula didn't have any problems with other Russians.

Following the imprisonment of Amuso in 1991, Casso became the de facto boss of the family. Anthony attempted to arrange for Amuso's escape from Federal custody after his arrest. To the great disappointment of Casso and the Lucchese captains, Amuso refused to leave prison out of fear for his life. As a result, the Lucchese captains asked Casso to replace him as boss, and Casso reluctantly accepted.

While evading authorities for over three years, Casso maintained control over the Lucchese family. In the process he ordered 11 mob slayings as well as plotting with Genovese leader Vincent "the Chin" Gigante to murder John Gotti. Casso and Gigante were deeply disgusted that Gotti had murdered Paul Castellano without the sanction of the "Mafia's Commission." All attempts on Gotti's life were stymied, however, by the constant presence of news reporters around the Gambino boss.

Vincente "The Chin" Gigante, a Genovese family leader who plotted with Casso to kill Gambino boss John Gotti.

Gambino boss John Gotti whose lavish ways as the "Teflon Don" made for a constant presence of news reporters which may have saved his life.

Law enforcement eventually caught up with the two fugitives. On July 29, 1991, the FBI captured Amuso in Pennsylvania, and in 1993 Casso was caught in Greenwood, New York. Amuso steadfastly refused all offers from the government to make a deal to become a government witness. In contrast, Casso quickly agreed to a deal and started revealing family secrets.

By this time, several high ranking members of the Luchesse family had been defected. Among them was a former captain whom Casso had targeted for assassination, Peter Chiodo. Chiodo had committed numerous murders for Casso, but was incensed that Casso had also ordered the assassination of his wife. According to Casso, Chiodo had chosen to involve his wife in the business of the Lucchese family. Therefore, he alone was responsible for the contract on her.

Once Casso realized that there was an enormous amount of evidence against him, he decided to become an informant. Believing that he would be sent into witness protection with his wife and children, Casso revealed everything he knew about the inner workings of the Lucchese Family. Casso disclosed that two NYPD detectives were on the Lucchese payroll. These detectives were later determined to be Louis Eppolito and Stephen Caracappa, who committed eight of the eleven murders, that Casso had ordered. Carracappa and Eppolito had also given Casso information which led to many others as well, revealing the names of potential informants. However, when Casso revealed similar corruption within the FBI, no one was interested. In addition, Casso also enraged federal prosecutors by accusing Gambino turncoat Sammy Gravano of masterminding Richard Kuklinski's murder of NYPD Detective Peter Calabro. Although this slaying was not covered by Gravano's immunity deal, no one was interested.

Peter Chiodo a former captain whom Casso had targeted for assassination. Chiodo had committed numerous murders for Casso, but was incensed that Casso had also ordered the assassination of his wife. According to Casso, Chiodo had chosen to involve his wife in the business of the Lucchese family. Therefore, he alone was responsible for the contract on her.

Two NYPD detectives who were on the Lucchese payroll. Louis Eppolito and Stephen Caracappa, who committed eight of the eleven murders Casso had ordered. Carracappa and Eppolito had also given Casso information which led to many others as well, revealing the names of potential. informants.

93 - Brooklyn Gangsters

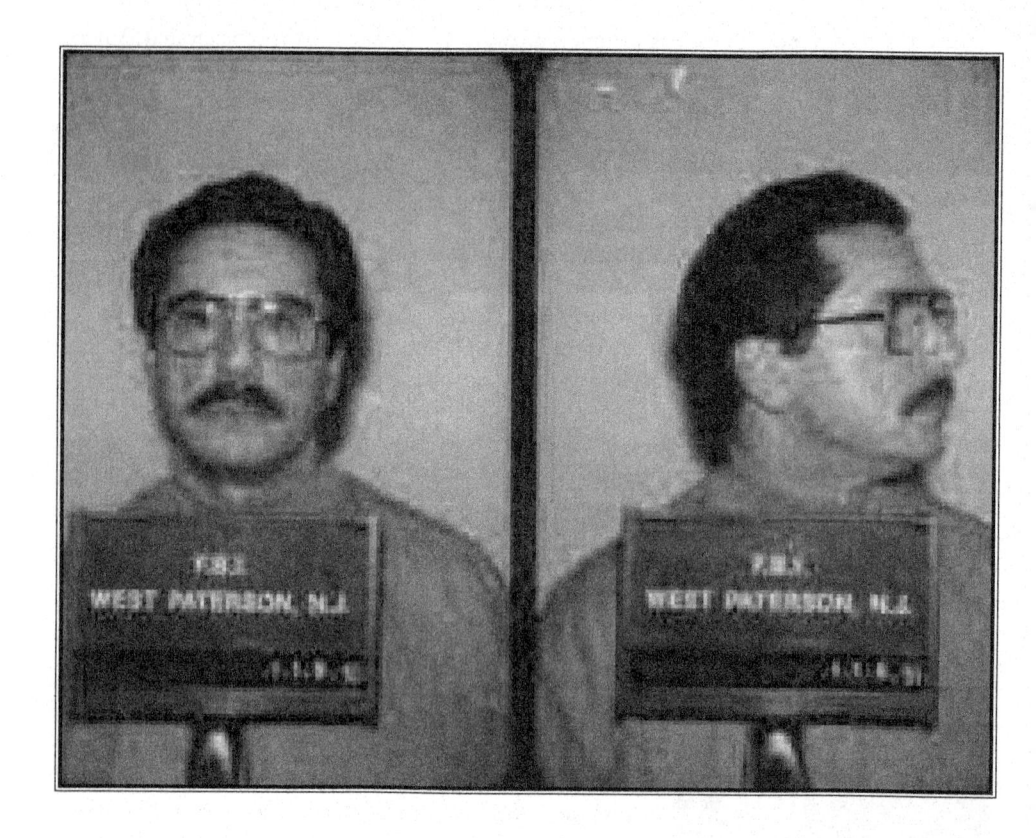

After his information was used to completely dismantle the Lucchese family, Casso was dropped from the Witness Protection Program. He is currently serving a life sentence without parole at the Supermax ADX Florence prison in Florence, Colorado.

Cusimano & Russo Funeral Home has been serving the families of Brooklyn since 1929 at 230 Court St.

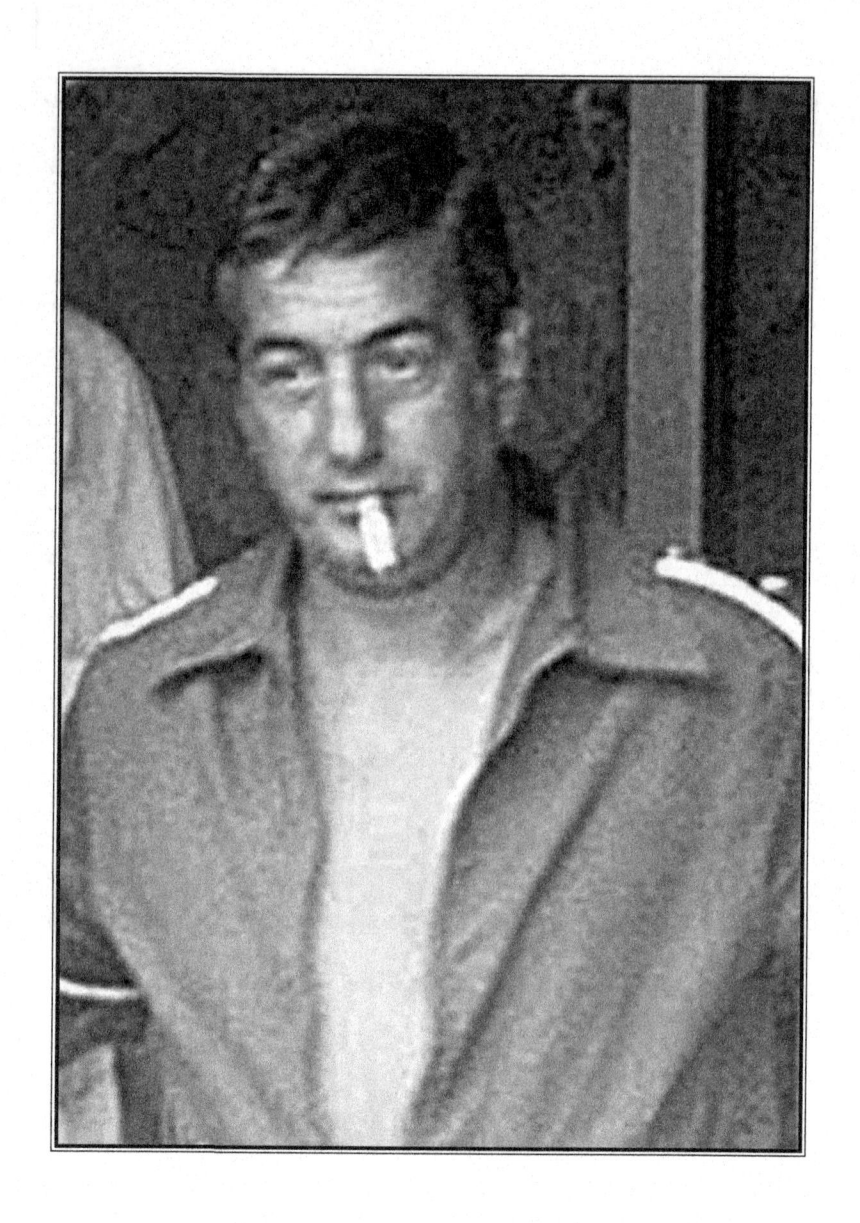

Dominick Napolitano
June 16, 1930 – August 17, 1981

DOMINICK NAPOLITANO
SONNY BLACK

Napolitano's parents were immigrants from Naples, Italy. Napolitano was born with blond hair, but by his forties it had turned a gunmetal white-silver color. To hide the color, he dyed it black, earning him the nickname "Sonny Black".

Napolitano was a sturdy 5'7" man who weighed about 170 pounds, with powerfully developed chest and arms. On his right forearm was a tattoo of a black panther. His face was fleshy, with dark brown eyes that made him look either tired or menacing. He was not a heavy drinker and only indulged at times, with fine French liquor. He had dead straight hair, a square jaw and a Roman nose. Napolitano controlled Greenpoint, Brooklyn from the 1960's to 1981.

Napolitano was an avid racing and homing pigeon enthusiast. He kept his collection of birds on the roof of his apartment and at his social club "The Motion Lounge." The brilliantly colored pigeons had pedigree bloodlines that descended from prize pigeons in France, Germany and Russia. Napolitano would win as much as $3,000 racing his pigeons.

Sonny was what you would call a colorful character, with a lot to prove. He became a "Captain" in the Bonanno Family around the late 70's and a force to contend with. Sonny's reputation grew to the point where he was welcomed to inter-family meetings, such as the one in the late 70's when Joe Massino was to meet high ranking members of the Gambino family to set up a contract. The contract was on Paul Castellano's daughter's boyfriend, Vito Borelli. It was important for Sonny to be there and show his face. This and many other instances helped elevate his position in the Bonanno Family. Sonny was a visionary of sorts, who tried to look beyond his Greenpoint, Brooklyn home for more profitable pastures. He held court at his bar, "The Motion Lounge," which the other Bonanno "capos" like John "Boobie" Cersani, Benjamin "Lefty" Ruggerio and Nicky Santora called home.

The Motion Lounge which many Bonanno family capos called home.

Benjamin "lefty" Ruggerio 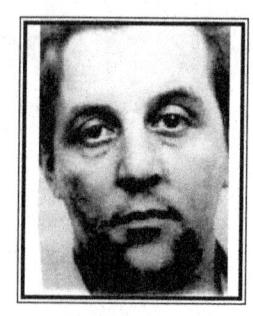   **Nicky Santora**    **Michael Sabella**

Napolitano was unusually tough and savvy, even for a "Mafia capo." Although he was a stone-cold gangster, he ran his crew in a laid-back style. Dominick was more observant and disciplined than his "old capo" Michael Sabella, and had a watchful eye. In mob circles, he had an excellent reputation for personal loyalty to his street soldiers. He would kill you in a minute if you crossed him. Napolitano was a fine marksman with most pistols, which made him an efficient killer.

Napolitano's headquarters "The Motion Lounge" located at 420 Graham Avenue, was in the heart of Williamsburg, Brooklyn, an Italian neighborhood. Napolitano also owned the "Wither's Italian-American War Veterans Club" at 415 Graham Avenue. His crew made a ton of money in burglary, extortion, robbery, bank robbery, loan sharking, hijacking, bookmaking, casino operations and drug trafficking, They were the most successful crews in the Bonanno family. Napolitano's other crew members included Nicholas Santora, Louis Attanasio, Jerome Asaro, Sandro Asaro, John Faraci, Daniel Mangelli, Robert Lino, Frank Lino, Richard Riccardi, Joseph Grimaldi, Nicholas Accardi, Peter Rosa, Patrick DeFillipo, Michael Mancuso, Vito Grimaldi, Anthony Urso, James Tartaglione, Joseph Cammarano, John Zancocchio, Edward Barberra, Frankie Fish, Bobby Badheart, Bobby Smash Joseph Puma, Steven Maruca, Salvatore Farrugia, Anthony Pesiri, Antonio Tomasulo, Anthony Rabito, Raymond Wean, Frank DiStefano, Salvatore D'Ottavio, James Episcopa, Donnie Brasco and his previous capo Michael Sabella. He also operated in Pasco County, Florida, and out of Holiday, Florida after negotiating control of the territory with Santo Trafficante Jr. At that time, Napolitano set his sights on operating a major bookmaking operation in Orlando. He would move forward with the aide of Donnie Brasco and open the "King's Court " restaurant/club in Florida. It acted as a front for the mob, and was a big accomplishment for Sonny, or so he thought. In the late 70's Tony Mirra, a "soldier" in the Bonanno crew, was introduced to a potential addition to the family. That potential addition was Donnie Brasco, who really was FBI agent Joseph Pistone. Tony Mirra brought him around everyone, and Benjamin Ruggerio ended up becoming his mentor in the Mafia. Benjamin was thrilled to find a possible protégé and soon would introduce him to Dominick "Sonny Black" Napolitano.

But it was an ill-fated idea. As Donnie's time in the crew grew, so did Sonny's trust for him. Sonny then took Donnie under his wing as an associate. This was the beginning of the end for both Benjamin and Sonny Black. Donnie's wheezing into the Mafia was a key to his infiltration of the Bonnano Family. At the time of his undercover work, a lot of leadership changes were brewing in the crime family. Sonny took over Mike Sabella's spot after the murder of Carmine "Lilo" Galante. This solidified his position with then boss Philip "Rusty" Rastelli. At this time a split occurred and the family became two rival factions. This caused Sonny to coordinate a security blanket on his crew with key movements in the family.

| Anthony Urso | Robert Lino | Frankie Lino | Donnie Brasco |

He was taped offering this "security blanket" on his crew with key movements in the family and offering this advice to Donnie Brasco on how to survive in the mob.

"The whole thing is how strong you are and how much power you got and how fucking mean you are—that's what makes you rise in the mob. Every day's a fucking struggle, because you don't know who's looking to knock you off, especially when you become a captain or boss. Every day, somebody's looking to dispose of you and take your position. You always got to be on your toes. Every fucking day is a scam day to keep your power and position."

Joseph Massino and Sonny Black were the chief masters of the sensational murder of the three rival "capos" Philip Giaccone, Alphonse "Red" Indelicato and Dominick "Trin" Trinchera in 1981. This only elevated Sonny's power and made him a force to be reckoned with. Donnie was at the center of this power struggle. Sonny's love and trust for Donnie grew and he proposed him for membership. With this new development Donnie was given a contract to carry out, the murder of Anthony "Bruno" Indelicato, to avoid retaliation.

The undercover work for Joseph Pistone would come to a screeching halt when the FBI learned of his possible induction and the murder contract. The FBI in turn went and informed the Bonanno Family of the breach. This, of course, sealed a death warrant against anyone involved in Joseph Pistone's entry into the family.

The clock was ticking for Sonny Black and a few others in the family. The first one to go was Tony Mirra who originally brought in Joseph Pistone. The next order came down to kill Napolitano for allowing an undercover agent into the family. On August 17, 1981, he was asked to come to a meeting in the basement of Bonanno associate Ron Filocomo's home in Flatlands, Brooklyn. Knowing he would be killed, Napolitano gave his jewelry to his favorite bartender who worked below his apartment at the "Motion Lounge," along with the keys to his apartment, so his pet pigeons could be cared for. Bonanno capo Frank Lino and Steven Cannone drove Napolitano to the house of Filocomo. Frank Coppa, was also present. Napolitano was pushed down the staircase in Filocomo's basement and shot to death by Filocomo, and Lino with .38 caliber revolvers. When the first shot misfired, Napolitano told them, "Hit me one more time and make it good".

Following this development Pistone was reached by Sonny's girlfriend who relayed a message that he held no ill-will against him that he knew that he was only doing his job. His death was hard for Pistone to swallow; he never meant for anyone to be killed due to his infiltration. Years later through the testimony of Frank Lino and Frank Coppa, they offered the details of Sonny's demise. Sonny would later be immortalized in the blockbuster film "Donnie Brasco".

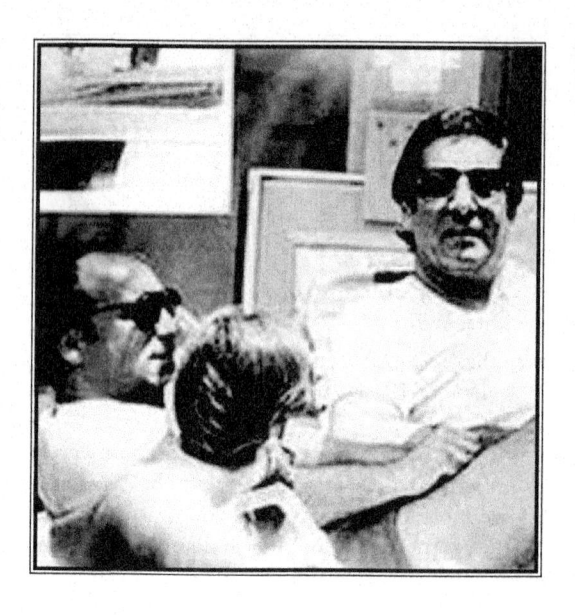

Now that we gave you a little background on Sonny, this is my problem with the story. I met Sonny in the early 70's. I used go the Motion Lounge with my Uncle Joey "Click Click." We used to play numbers there and have a few drinks. I used to hang around Sonny and some of the crew, and I never found him to be a nasty guy. I happened to like him. I'm not saying what he did in his life is right, but he did it. What I don't like is an undercover cop that sets guys up, not that the guys would not have committed crimes anyway, but having the law bring scores to you and to be part of it on the notion that they are doing something that's right, isn't it like giving a junkie dope.? The law knew that they were putting those guy's lives on the line, and that's exactly what happened. They got them killed, Sonny and Tony. The law was smart enough to get Donnie in and commit crimes with the boys, but that's ok, it's for the law. They just should have assassinated them instead of spending millions on this covert mission. I read the book Donnie Brasco and I think its all bullshit. I would have liked to read all the shit they covered up and the crimes they committed to pull this off. Donnie knew damn well while he was on the inside that his friends were going to get killed. He said he felt bad but "it's his job." Getting guys killed is a job? Well I feel bad too when I run over a stray cat by accident. What the fuck does that mean? If I knew I was going to run over that cat on that street I would go a different way, but that's me, and it's a cat not an Italian gangster. The cat would have gotten more respect by the law than Sonny and Tony did.

The gravesite of Dominick Napolitano at Cavalry Cemetary in New York.

For the best kishke and a 10 inch hotdog, Kishke King was the place to go at 1711 Pitkins Avenue, Brooklyn. Its long gone like most good things.

John Joseph Gotti Jr.
October 27, 1940 – June 10, 2002

JOHN GOTTI
THE DAPPER DON

John Joseph Gotti Jr, was an American mobster who became the "Boss" of the Gambino crime family in New York City. He was the fifth of thirteen children of John Joseph Gotti Sr. and his wife Philomena (referred to as Fannie). When John was a child, the Gottis lived on 2282 Dean Street in East New York, Brooklyn.

Gotti grew up in poverty. His father worked irregularly as a day laborer and indulged in gambling, and as an adult Gotti came to resent him for being unable to provide for his family. In school Gotti had a history of truancy and bullying other students and ultimately dropped out, while attending Franklin K. Lane High School at the age of 16.

Gotti married Victoria DiGiorgio on March 6, 1962. The marriage produced five children—two daughters (Angel and Victoria) as well as three sons (John, Frank and Peter). Gotti attempted to work legitimately in 1962 as a presser in a coat factory and as an assistant truck driver. However, he could not stay crime free and by 1966 had been jailed twice.

Franklin K. Lane High School, where Gotti bullied other students and eventually dropped out at age 16.

A young John Gotti Jr. posing for a mug shot.

104 - Brooklyn Gangsters

On March 18, 1980, Gotti's youngest son, 12-year-old Frank Gotti, was run over and killed on a family friend's mini bike by John Favara, a neighbor. While Frank's death was ruled an accident, Favara subsequently received death threats. He tried to visit the Gottis to apologize to no avail. He was told by John's crew to leave but he didn't. On July 28, 1980 while the Gottis were on vacation in Florida, Favara was abducted and disappeared, presumed murdered. John Gotti is still presumed to have ordered the killing, an allegation considered probable by his son John Jr., while denied by his daughter Victoria.

Gotti was involved in street gangs associated with "New York Mafioso" from the age of 12. When he was 14, after leaving school, he devoted himself to working with the "Fulton-Rockaway Boys," a local gang where he met and befriended fellow future Gambino mobsters Angelo Ruggiero and Wilfred "Willie Boy" Johnson.

Gambino mobsters Angelo Ruggiero (left) and Wilfred "Willie Boy" Johnson (right).

He and his brothers started operating out of the Ozone Park neighborhood of Queens. Gotti quickly rose in prominence, becoming one of the crime family's biggest earners and a protégé of Gambino family under boss Aniello Dellacroce.

Gotti's criminal career began when he joined Carmine Fatico's crew, which was part of what became known as the Gambino family after the murder of Albert Anastasia. Together with his brother Gene and Ruggiero, Gotti carried out truck hijackings at Idlewild Airport, later renamed John F. Kennedy International Airport.

Gambino under boss Aniello Dellacroce.

During this time, Gotti befriended fellow mob hijacker and future Bonanno family boss Joseph Massino. In February 1968, United Airlines employees identified Gotti as the man who had signed for stolen merchandise; the FBI arrested him for the United hijacking soon after. Two months later, while out on bail, Gotti was arrested a third time for hijacking on the New Jersey Turnpike—this time for stealing a load of cigarettes worth $50,000. Later that year, Gotti pleaded guilty to the Northwest Airlines hijacking and was sentenced to three years at Lewisburg Federal Penitentiary. Prosecutors dropped the charges for the cigarette hijacking. Gotti also pleaded guilty to the United hijacking and spent less than three years at Lewisburg.

Bonanno family boss, Joseph Massino.

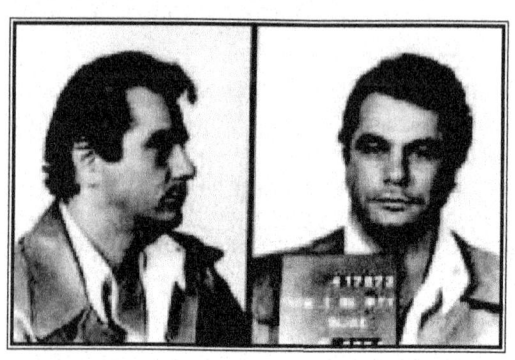

John Gotti posing for a mug shot.

After he was released from prison, Gotti was placed on probation and ordered to acquire legitimate employment. Meanwhile, he returned to his old crew at the Bergin Hunt and Fish Club, still working under "capo" regime Carmine Fatico. Fatico was indicted on loan sharking charges in 1972 and made Gotti, (still not yet a made man in the Mafia,) the acting "capo" of the Bergin Crew, reporting to Carlo Gambino and his under boss, Aniello Dellacroce. After Carlo Gambino's nephew Emanuel Gambino was kidnapped and murdered, John Gotti was assigned to the hit team alongside Ralph Galione and Angelo Ruggiero for the main suspect, Irish-American gangster James McBratney. The team botched their attempt to abduct McBratney at a Staten Island bar, and Galione shot McBratney dead. Identified by eyewitnesses and a police street rat, Gotti was arrested for the killing in June 1974 with the help of attorney Roy Cohn; however, he was able to strike a plea bargain and received a four-year sentence for attempted manslaughter for his part in the hit.

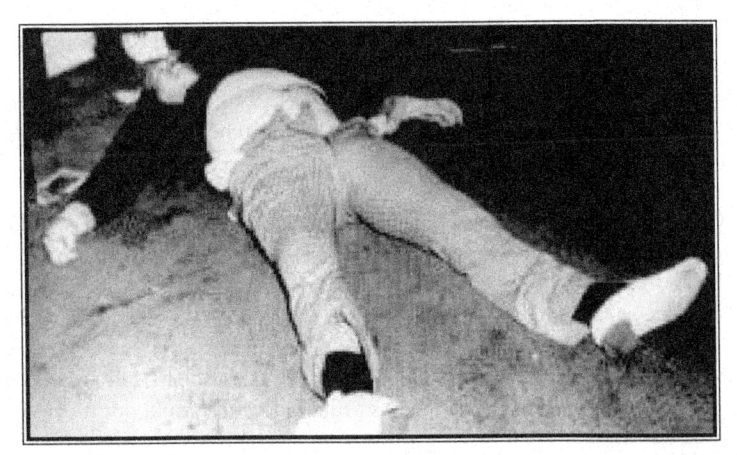

A picture of the slain James McBratney, who was shot by Ralph Galione, but who Gotti was arrested for killing. Gotti, along with his lawyers, was able to work the charges down to only four years.

Gotti was released in July 1977 after two years in prison. When he got out he was initiated into the Gambino family, now under the command of Paul Castellano, and immediately promoted to replace Fatico as Capo of the Bergin crew. He and his crew reported directly to Dellacroce as part of the concessions given by Castellano to keep Dellacroce as under boss, and Gotti was regarded as Dellacroce's protégé.

Under Gotti, the Bergin crew were the biggest earners of Dellacroce's crews. Besides his cut of his subordinates' earnings, Gotti ran his own loan sharking operation and held a no-show job as a plumbing supply salesman.

After the FBI indicted members of Gotti's crew for selling narcotics, Gotti took advantage of growing dissent over the leadership of the crime family. Fearing that he and his men would be killed by Gambino crime family boss Paul Castellano for selling drugs, Gotti organized the murder of Castellano in December 1985 and took over the family shortly thereafter. This left Gotti as the boss of the most powerful crime family in America, which made hundreds of millions of dollars a year from construction, hijacking, loan sharking, gambling, extortion and other criminal activities. Gotti was the most powerful crime boss during his era and became widely known for his outspoken personality and flamboyant style, which eventually helped lead to his downfall. While his peers would go out of their way to avoid the media, Gotti was known as the "The Dapper Don" for his expensive clothes and personality in front of news cameras. He was later given the nickname "The Teflon Don" because several attempts to convict him of crimes in the 1980's resulted in either a hung jury or an acquittal.

Boss of Gambino crime family who iniated Gotti into the family, Paul Castellano.

Gotti rapidly became dissatisfied with Paul Castellano's leadership, considering the new boss to be isolated and greedy.

In August 1983 Ruggiero and Gene Gotti were arrested for dealing heroin, based primarily on recordings from a "bug" in Ruggiero's house. Castellano, who had banned "made men" in his family from dealing drugs under threat of death, demanded transcripts of the tapes, and when Ruggiero refused he threatened to demote Gotti.

In 1984 Castellano was arrested and indicted in a RICO case for the crimes of Gambino hit man Roy DeMeo's crew. The following year he received a second indictment for his role in the American Mafia's Commission. Facing life imprisonment for both cases, Castellano arranged for John Gotti to serve as an acting boss alongside Thomas Bilotti, Castellano's favorite capo, and Thomas Gambino in his absence. Gotti, meanwhile, began conspiring with fellow disgruntled Gambino family members Sammy Gravano, Frank DeCicco, Robert DiBernardo and Joseph Armone to overthrow Castellano. Gotti made a promise that he would not move on Castellano until Dellacroce was dead.

Gene Gotti 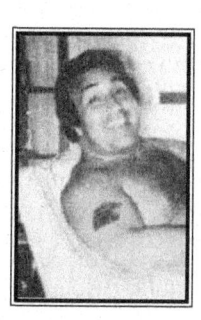 **Thomas Bilotti**  **Sammy Gravano**  **Frank DeCicco**

After Dellacroce died of cancer on December 2, 1985, Castellano revised his succession plan, appointing Bilotti as under boss to Thomas Gambino as the sole acting boss, while making plans to break up Gotti's crew. Infuriated by this and by Castellano's refusal to attend Dellacroce's wake, Gotti resolved to kill his boss.

Gotti agreed to a meeting with Castellano and Bilotti at "Sparks Steak House" on December 16, 1985. When the boss and under boss arrived, they were ambushed and shot dead by assassins under Gotti's command. Gotti watched the hit from his car with Gravano.

Gotti was proclaimed the new boss of the Gambino family at the meeting of the "family's capos" on December 30, 1983. He appointed his co-conspirator DeCicco as the new under boss while retaining Castellano's consigliere Joseph N. Gallo.

Identified as both Paul Castellano's likely murderer and his successor, John Gotti rose to fame throughout 1986.

Gotti's new fame had at least one positive effect; with some intimidation by the Gambino's hoods, Romual Piecyk, who was testifying against Gotti in assault charges, had decided not to testify against Gotti. When the trial commenced in March 1986, he testified that he was unable to remember who attacked him. The case was promptly dismissed, with the New York Daily News summarizing the proceedings with the headline "I Forgotti!". On April 13, 1986, under boss DeCicco was killed when his car was bombed following a visit to Castellano loyalist James Failla. The bombing was carried out by Lucchese capos Victor Amuso and Anthony Casso, under orders of bosses Anthony Corallo and Vincent Gigante to avenge Castellano and Bilotti by killing their successors; Gotti also planned to visit Failla that day but canceled, and the bomb was detonated after a soldier who rode with DeCicco was mistaken for the boss. The use of bombs was banned by the American Mafia. Since Casso and Amuso used a bomb, "it was a style used in Sicily," it cleared Gigante of suspicion from Gotti.

Following the bombing, Judge Eugene Nickerson, presiding over Gotti's racketeering trial, rescheduled to August 1992 to avoid a jury tainted by the resulting publicity, while Giacalone had Gotti's bail revoked due to evidence of intimidation in the Piecyk case. From jail, Gotti ordered the murder of Robert DiBernardo by Sammy Gravano, having been told by Ruggiero that DiBernardo had challenged his leadership. The real reason was "Sammy the Bull" wanted to take over Dibernardo's lucrative business and used this as the excuse. He also had Joseph Armone promoted to replace DeCicco.

On December 11, 1990, FBI agents and New York City detectives raided the "Ravenite Social Club," arresting Gotti, Gravano and Frank Locascio. Gotti was charged, in this new racketeering case, with five murders (Castellano and Bilotti, Robert DiBernardo, Liborio Milito and Louis Dibono,) conspiracy to murder Gaetano "Corky" Vastola, loan sharking, illegal gambling, obstruction of justice, bribery and tax evasion. Based on tapes from FBI "bugs" played at pretrial hearings, the Gambino administration was denied bail, and attorneys Bruce Cutler and Gerald Shargel were both disqualified from defending Gotti after determining they had worked as "in-house counsel" for the Gambino organization. Gotti subsequently hired Albert Kriegra, a Miami attorney who had worked with Joseph Bonanno, to replace Cutler.

Gaetano "Corky" Vastola, who was arrested along with Sammy "the bull" Gravano after FBI agents raided the Ravenite Social Club.

The Raventite Social Club, where several of Gotti's men were arrested.

The tapes also created a rift between Gotti and Gravano, showing the Gambino boss describing his newly-appointed under boss as too greedy and attempting to frame Gravano as the main force behind the murders of DiBernardo, Milito and Dibono. Gravano, knowing he was a dead man if he beat the case, ultimately opted to turn state's evidence, formally agreeing to testify on November 13, 1991.

Gotti and Locascio were tried in the United States District Court for the Eastern District of New York before United States District Judge I. Leo Glasser. Jury selection began in January 1992, with the empaneled jury being kept anonymous and, for the first time in a Brooklyn Federal case, fully sequestered during the trial due to Gotti's reputation for jury tampering. The trial commenced with the prosecution's opening statements on February 12th. Prosecutors Andrew Maloney and John Gleeson began their case by playing tapes showing Gotti discussing Gambino family business, including murders he approved, and confirming the animosity between Gotti and Castellano to establish the former's motive to kill his boss. After calling an eyewitness of the Sparks hit who identified Gotti associate John Carneglia as one of the men who shot Bilotti, they then brought Gravano to testify on March 2.

Gotti's under boss Salvatore "Sammy the Bull" Gravano is credited with the FBI's success in finally convicting Gotti. In 1991, Gravano agreed to turn state's evidence and testify for the prosecution against Gotti after hearing Gotti on wiretap make several disparaging remarks and questioning his loyalty.

On the stand Gravano confirmed Gotti's "place" in the structure of the Gambino family and described in detail the conspiracy to assassinate Castellano and gave a full description of the hit, and its aftermath. Krieger and Locasio's attorney Anthony Cardinale, proved unable to shake Gravano during cross-examination. After additional testimony and tapes, the government rested its case on March 24.

John Gotti, and brother Peter Gotti.

Five of Krieger and Cardinale's intended six witnesses were ruled irrelevant or extraneous, leaving only Gotti's tax attorney Murray Appleman to testify on his behalf. The defense also attempted unsuccessfully to have a mistrial declared based on Maloney's closing remarks. Gotti himself became increasingly hostile during the trial, and at one point Glasser threatened to remove him from the courtroom. Among other outbursts, Gotti called Gravano a junkie while his attorneys sought to discuss Gravano's past steroid use.

On April 2, 1992, after only 14 hours of deliberation, the jury found Gotti guilty on all charges of the indictment (Locasio was found guilty on all but one). On June 23, 1992, Glasser sentenced both defendants to life imprisonment without parole and a $250,000 fine.

Gotti was incarcerated at the United States Penitentiary at Marion, Illinois. He spent the majority of his sentence in effective solitary confinement, only being allowed out of his cell for one hour a day.

Despite his imprisonment, and pressure from the Commission to stand down, Gotti is believed to have held on to his position as Gambino boss with his brother Peter and his son John A. Gotti Jr. relaying orders on his behalf. By 1998, when he was indicted on racketeering, John Gotti Jr. was believed to be the acting boss of the family. Against his father's wishes, John Jr. pleaded guilty and was sentenced to six years and five months imprisonment in 1999. He maintains he has since left the Gambino family.

In 1998 Gotti was diagnosed with throat cancer and sent to the United States Medical Center for Federal Prisoners in Springfield, Missouri for surgery. While the tumor was removed, the cancer was discovered to have returned two years later and Gotti was transferred back to Springfield, where he would spend the remainder of his life. Gotti's condition rapidly declined, and he died on June 10, 2002 at the age of 61. The Roman Catholic Diocese of Brooklyn announced that Gotti's family would not be permitted to have a Mass of Christian burial but allowed it after the burial.

Gotti's funeral was held in a non-church facility. After the funeral, an estimated 300 onlookers followed the procession, which passed Gotti's "Bergin Hunt and Fish Club," to the grave site. Gotti was buried next to his son Frank Gotti.

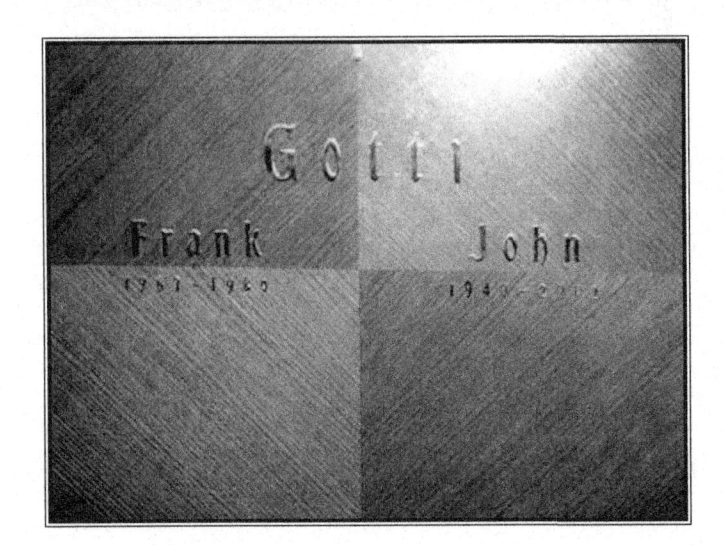

One short note..... I met John Gotti on Court Street at a restaurant and had lunch with him and his bodyguard Bobby Boreillo, a childhood friend of mine who used to be with the Gallo family before asking for a release to go with Gotti. As I sat with John and Bobby and a glass of wine, Bobby told John that I was Ricky's son so John would allow me in. After a half hour of John ranting about the case and how the law was trying to do anything to fry him, it was time to go. As we gave each other a kiss goodbye, he whispered in my ear "tell you father it was a mistake with Debe and to watch the guys around him"..... "What a trip!"

The Cyclone opened on June 26, 1927, a ride cost only twenty-five cents. In 1935, the Rosenthals took over management. The ride continued to be extremely popular; the roller coaster was completely rehabilitated and opened to enthusiastic crowds on July 1, 1975. It's still the best around, located at 834 Surf Avenue and West 10th Street, Coney Island, Brooklyn.

BROOKLYN GANGSTERS WE CAN'T LEAVE OUT

Louis Capone
unknown, 1896 - March 4, 1944

LOUIS CAPONE
THE ESPRESSO KING

One of the greatest mistakes so-called "mob experts" make is confusing Meyer Lansky and Bugsy Siegel with the "goings on" of Lepke Buchalter and Gurrah Shapiro in their running of the Brownsville organization known as "Murder Incorporated." Lansky and Siegel were underlings of primary organized crime family boss, Lucky Luciano. The "Sicilian" Luciano and "Neapolitan" Costello, were among the first to have working relationships with Jewish gangsters, and as a result wound up with major Jewish associates in their crew. Most of those Jews were part of the organization that answered to Lansky, and to a lesser degree, Siegel, who was less of a team player. Guys like the Rosenbergs, Sam and Ralph "Beaky" (Beaky was later accused of killing the black owner of Queens nightclub, Conrad's Cloud Room) and Max "The Jew" Shrager, whose son Ian went on to co-own the infamous Studio 54, became a rat, then went on to own a chain of chic hotels that include the "Delano" in Miami Beach and the "Mondrian" in Los Angeles.

Across the river in Brownsville, Brooklyn, was the gang known as "Murder Incorporated." It was run at the top by Albert Anastasia, his underling Louis "Lepke" Buchalter and finally by Louis Capone, an Ocean Hill wiseguy in Anastasia's family. Capone had an Italian pastry café in Ocean Hill, close to Brownsville, where youngsters Abe "Kid Twist" Reles and "Happy" Maione (another myth was that "Murder Incorporated" was all Jewish) hung out and received the tutelage of the Anastasia wiseguy. Capone encouraged the two, who were often at odds, to pull together the other young toughs they hung out with, into an enforcement, and earning arm of the Anastasia crime family, and "Murder Incorporated" was born.

The dapper and exquisitely groomed Capone's claim to fame was a close connection with the "Purple Gang" of Detroit, and he was, in fact, involved with them in a shylock operation that blanketed a good part of the nation. Though they had the same last name, Louis Capone was not related to "Scarface" Al Capone, of Chicago. Louis Capone's "pasticceria" was not a hub of criminal activity just because of his cannolis and espresso, but because of his boss, Albert Anastasia, and other members of what was then the crime family of Vincent Mangano and his brother Philip.

Between Capone's nationwide network and his group of "Murder Incorporated" killers, he began to take contracts from other families and even other cities to bring money to the Mangano-Anastasia's coffers. When, in 1936, Lepke Buchalter had trouble with a trucker who was giving his top union operative, Max Rubin, a hard time, and was rumored to be talking to the authorities about mob control in garment center trucking, Lepke ordered him killed. The order went to Louis Capone, who in turn, made sure it was taken care of. When "Kid Twist" went bad and testified for prosecutor Burton Turkus about, among other things, the murder of trucker Joe Rosen, Lepke Buchalter, his hulking bodyguard, Mendy Weiss, and Louis Capone were convicted and sentenced to death.

On March 4, 1944, Louis Capone was electrocuted in the chair at Sing Sing prison, in Ossining, New York. Buchalter and Weiss followed him to that doom.

Farrell's bar is the real McCoy, dating back to 1933, when Park Slope was Irish. They've finally added stools, but there's still no table service. Ordering a "large" will get you a 32-ounce Styrofoam bucket. This place is old school at 215 Prospect Park West, Brooklyn.

117 - Brooklyn Gangsters

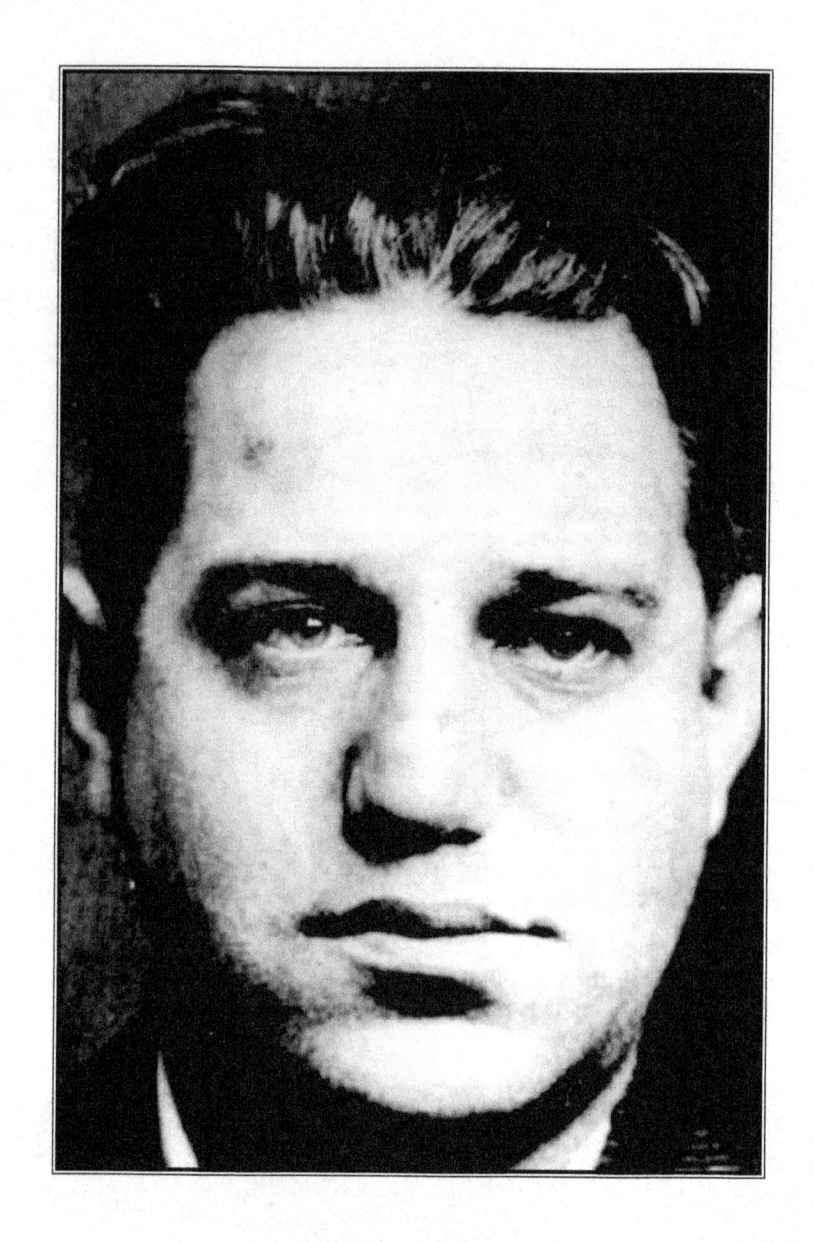

Seymour Magoon
Born, unknown - Death, unknown

SEYMOUR MAGOON
BLUE JAW

He was said to be the toughest killer in "Murder Incorporated," tougher than even the sadistic psychopath Harry "Pittsburgh Phil" Strauss. But in the end, Seymour "Blue Jaw" Magoon turned out to be just another "canary."

Magoon got the moniker "Blue Jaw" because he looked like he always was in need of a shave. Of Irish decent, Magoon grew up in the mean streets of Brownsville, Brooklyn, and quit school at an early age. "Fourteen or sixteen was when I left school," Magoon later said. "I'm not sure. You see I wasn't interested in school much." By 1933, Magoon had already shot two men, but to him that didn't count. "They were only wounded," he said.

Magoon quickly caught the eye of Louie "Lepke" Buchalter, and was inserted as one of Lepke's top killers, along with Strauss, Abe "Kid Twist" Reles, "Buggsy" Goldstein, "Happy" Maione, "Dasher" Abbandando, "Dandy Jack" Parisi and Allie Tannenbaum, in a group graciously called "Murder Incorporated." Magoon was the best driver of the bunch, so although he was as capable a shooter as anyone in the group, his usual job was to handle the getaway car after a big hit. All the shooters were given weekly retainers by Lepke, estimated to be one thousand dollars per week. But after an especially big "piece of work," Lepke was not adverse to paying them an added bonus.

Even though Strauss and Reles were stone killers, Magoon would take "guff" off none of them. "I can take care of myself," Magoon would say to anyone who would listen.

Once Magoon and homicidal Strauss got into a beef over a killing, "You can't talk to me like that," Magoon told Strauss. Those in attendance figured Strauss, who enjoyed killing as much as he loved his mother, and he loved his mother a lot, would murder Magoon on the spot. Yet it was Strauss who backed off, even apologizing to Magoon, who had murder in his eyes too.

As for Reles, even though they worked together often, Magoon didn't care for "Kid Twist" too much either. "Reles is mean and cheap," Magoon told one of his fellow killers. "When he's with his superiors in the mob, he wines and dines them, and makes a show at splurging. With his equals, or subordinates, he argues when it's time to pay a check."

After almost a decade of murder, the boys were "done in" because of a hit gone wrong. On July 25, 1939, at 7:55 am, Magoon sat behind the wheel of a sedan parked in front of 250 E. 178 th Street. in the Bronx. Sitting next to him was "Dandy Jack" Parisi and in the back seat was a small-time hood named Jacob "Kuppy" Migden, who had spent a week tailing the the intended target. Suddenly, a short, stocky man came out of the building and Migden said, "That's him!" Magoon put the car in gear and slowly passed their mark. Then he made an easy U-turn, and Parisi stepped out onto the running board and pumped six 32 caliber bullets into the man's back. The only problem was, Midgen had identified the wrong man.

The dead man turned out to be Irving Penn, a 42-year-old executive with G. Schirmer Inc., a Manhattan classical music publisher. The intended target was Philip Orlovsky, a former garment union boss, who was ready to rat on his ex-partner, "Murder Incorporated's" top man, Louie "Lepke". Unfortunately for the now dead Penn, he lived in the same building as Orlovsky. The men looked somewhat alike, but Penn was seventy five pounds heavier and wore eyeglasses. Orlovsky was alive only because he had left his apartment an hour earlier to get a haircut and a shave.

The local newspapers had a field day with this one, gleefully reporting on the gruesome murder of a man who just happened to be in the wrong place at the wrong time. Lepke gave orders to all his killers, who could tie Lepke to hundreds of murders, to go on the lam, someplace far far away, until the heat cooled down (which turned out to be never), or until Lepke himself was dead. Magoon split with "Buggsy" Goldstein by car on a cross-country trip that led them through Canada, Kansas City, California, Mexico, then back east, until they settled in a known mob hideaway in Newburgh, New York.

One day, Goldstein trekked into town to pick up a money order that had been wired to them, but the cops were waiting and put the handcuffs on Goldstein. In jail, he tried to slip a note to Magoon, telling him to split quick, but the law intercepted the note and arrested Magoon at their hideout. Magoon tried to tell the police his name was Harry Levinson, and when they showed him a mug shot of Goldstein, he said he looked familiar, but couldn't place him. Because they had nothing concrete on Magoon, they gave him 60 days in the slammer for "vagrancy."

While he was cooling his heels in the can, Magoon found out that Goldstein had been indicted for murder and that Reles had decided to become a rat against Goldstein. This did not please Magoon the least bit. "It looks like I'm on my way, unless I get into the act," Magoon told the "fuzz." "I better find a peg to hang my hat on too."

Magoon's old pals Strauss and Goldstein were tried together for assorted murders and mayhem. Reles took the stand for several days, putting countless nails in his former partners' coffins. But it was Magoon who put the finishing touches on the trial, when he took the stand and revealed all he knew about every murder Strauss and Goldstein had been involved with, and there were plenty. While Magoon was babbling away in front of the jury, Goldstein jumped to his feet and screamed "For God sake, Seymour, that's some story you're telling. You're burning me."

And burn him he did. Both Strauss and Goldstein were convicted and died in the electric chair soon after, at Sing Sing Prison. Magoon did a few years in the slammer, but then disappeared from the face of the earth, or at least from Brownsville. There is no record of the time and cause of his death. But in 2003, more than 60 years after he turned "canary", Magoon's skeleton was found in a desert near Las Vegas.

Union Street Meat Market was established in 1945 and is still family owned. I went to get meat for my grandparents every day as a kid and it still looks the same as it did then. Located at 353 Union on the corner of Smith Street, Brooklyn.

Harry Strauss
July 28, 1909 – June 12, 1941

HARRY STRAUSS
PITTSBURGH PHIL

Harry Strauss, who called himself "Pittsburgh Phil," was the most cold-blooded killer our country has ever seen. Strauss started out as a small-time hood in the Brownsville section of Brooklyn, and he was soon famous for being an efficient contract killer, who never carried a weapon unless he was "on a job." Strauss, who had never been to Pittsburgh in his life (he just liked the name), was called "Pep" by his homicidal associates. He liked committing murder so much (it was reported he killed anywhere from one hundred to five hundred people), he often volunteered for murder contracts, as Brooklyn District Attorney William O'Dwyer once said, "just for the lust to kill."

Strauss was so good at his "job," other big-time mobsters began to take notice. Strauss explained, "Like a ballplayer, that's me. I figure I get my seasoning doing these jobs. Someone from one of those big mobs spots me, then, up to the Big Leagues."

That is exactly what eventually happened. In the early 1930's, Strauss caught the eye of Louie "Lepke" Buchalter, who had just formed his group of trained contract killers called "Murder Incorporated." Strauss was invited into the "Big Leagues," and soon Strauss' murder output exceeded those of "Murder Incorporated's" next two most prolific killers, "Happy" Maione and Abe Relles, combined. When an out-of-town contract was required, it was almost always Strauss who was requested. When those occasions arose, Strauss packed a bag with a shirt, change of socks, underwear, a gun, length of rope and an ice pick, just in case. Most times, Strauss didn't even know the name of the man whom he had killed, and didn't care anyway. Still, Strauss sometimes got copies of the newspaper of the city in which he had recently finished a contract, just to "admire the efficiency" of his handiwork.

As proficient as he was at killing, Strauss was just as good in the art of seducing members of the opposite sex. Tall, dark and handsome, Strauss wore $60 suits, which in the time of the Depression, was a kingly sum. Once, while he was in a lineup at a local police station, New York City Police Commissioner Lewis Valentine remarked, "Look at him! He's the best dressed man in the room and he's never worked a day in his life." Strauss had a steamy love affair with Brooklyn beauty Evelyn Middleman, who was called "The Kiss of Death," because in order to win her affections, Strauss had to murder her former boyfriend.

Once, during the course of a hit, Strauss injured himself, and as a result, he made his victims death all the more gruesome. One night, Strauss and a few of his confederates lured "Puggy" Feinstein into a Brooklyn home where Strauss commenced stabbing Feinstein numerous times with an ice-pick. But Feinstein would not go away easily and he bit down hard on Strauss' pinkie finger, almost severing the mangled digit. "Give me a rope. I'll fix this bum," Strauss said. With the help of his pals, Strauss formed a noose with the rope and put it around Feinstein's neck. He tied the other end of the rope around Feinstein's feet, trussing him up like a Thanksgiving Day turkey. Then they gleefully watched, as Feinstein struggled frantically, slowly strangling himself to death.

After Feinstein took his last breath, they dragged him to a nearby vacant lot and used his body to start a bon fire. They resisted the urge to roast marshmallows, instead, absconded to a Sheepshead Bay restaurant to celebrate. While the boys were chowing down their hardy meal, Strauss was none too happy. When asked what was wrong, Strauss said, "Maybe I'm getting lockjaw from being bit." He hardly finished his lobster dinner.

Not all of Strauss' contract hits went according to plan. Once he was summoned down to Jacksonville, Florida to do a "piece of work," for the local mob boss. His contact in Jacksonville took Strauss to the mark's house and told him the hit would be an easy one, because the man left his home every day at exactly the same time. But Strauss didn't like the set-up. The target's house was on a busy two-way street corner and there was no expert wheelman, or even a getaway car to flee the scene after the deed was done. So Strauss decided to follow the mark, and that he did, first to a busy restaurant, then to a nearby movie house.

When Strauss entered the movie house, he was happy to see that his man had taken a seat in the back row, all by himself. Strauss was then overjoyed, when he looked to his right and spotted an ax in a glass case, with the sign under it saying, "To be used in case of a fire." Strauss felt as if the ax had been placed there by the "hand of God."

Strauss took the ax from its case and slowly made his way to where his "mark" was sitting. Then suddenly, a lady stood up from one of the front row seats and exited the movie house. Strauss' intended target immediately jumped to his feet and hurried to the empty seat up front. Convinced this job was jinxed, Strauss put the ax back into its case and exited the movie house. He went back to his hotel, packed quickly, headed for the airport and high-tailed it back to Brooklyn. He explained to his confederates why the hit went awry.

"Those Florida jerks wanted me to do a cowboy job," Strauss said. "And then just when I go set him up properly, the bum turns out to be a God-damned chair-hopper."

Speaking of chairs, after Abe Reles squealed to the cops on his confederates at "Murder Incorporated," on June 12, 1941, Strauss was given the chair himself, the electric chair at Sing Sing Prison, at exactly 11:06 pm Eastern Standard Time, thereby elevating Strauss from the "Big Leagues," to the "Posthumous Hit Man Hall of Fame."

The gravesite of Harry Strauss.

Red Rose Restaurant. Many people think that it opened in the 1980's but it's been there since the 1940's. The Gallo Boys hung out there in the 60's and 70's. I used to meet Roy Musico once a week, but maybe it's better nobody knows that. It's located at 315 Smith St., Brooklyn.

Louis Amberg
unknown, 1897 – October 23, 1935

LOUIS AMBERG
PRETTY

Think of the ugliest person you know...someone whose face would scare the life out of you if you met him on a dark street. Someone whose face would scare you into sobriety if you saw it while your alcohol level was elevated. Would you call him Pretty? Short and "looks-challenged" Louis Amberg (who had once been offered a job with the circus to be billed as "The Missing Link") was dubbed "Pretty" by the people who knew him best. Those people were the Brownsville, Brooklyn residents, including the professional murderers known by the group name of Murder Incorporated. When an inebriated Mayor Jimmy Walker saw Pretty in a speakeasy one night during Prohibition, he instantly swore never to drink again.

Pointy-eared, beady-eyed, mole ridden and scarred, Pretty Amberg was as mean as he was ugly. He was nasty to strangers, sometimes knocking plates off their tables as he walked through a restaurant, telling them to order different food. Everyone hated Pretty, who was known to leave his murder victims, (estimated to surpass one hundred), in laundry bags mostly on the streets of Brownsville. For residents of an area not accustomed to bodies turning up with abnormal frequency, Pretty Amberg was someone to be exceptionally feared. One person who seemed to be able to find a loveable side to him was his girlfriend, a seventeen year old actress known by the stage name of Rita Rio, who claimed she didn't know of Pretty's profession or reputation. Was it the money and gifts he showered on her that blinded Rita, or did she really need strong eyeglasses?

After having had dozens of "Moustache Petes" murdered in the second "Night of the Vespers," high level mobsters like Lucky Luciano, Frank Costello and Joe Bonnano were trying to keep order in their new form of organized crime. Yet "tough-as-nails" Amberg was a loose cannon who threatened other criminals and killed connected gangsters without consulting higher ups. Those actions threatened all they had worked for. Pretty Amberg was a pain in the ass. He did some contract "work" for "Murder Incorporated," but was not officially part of that group, which operated under the auspices of Lepke Buchalter and Albert Anastasia. He was given a "go ahead" to collect money from Abe "Kid Twist" Reles in a beef where he was obviously wrong. Mediators Bugsy Siegel, Joe Adonis and the aforementioned Albert Anastasia wanted to lull Pretty into a place where he would trust them enough to meet them when they called. Unwittingly, he was tied to Dutch Schultz, who was the person he was most closely associated with, in a more profound way than he ever imagined.

Once, when Schultz teasingly threatened to open a craps game directly across the street from Pretty's Court Street casino, the latter told Dutch to put a gun into his own mouth and see how many times he could fire it. He told Schultz that killing himself would afford him a better end than he would have if he messed with him. It turned out that Pretty met his end on the same night that Lucky Luciano's men murdered Dutch Schultz at the Palace Chop House, in New Jersey. He was "disposed of" for insisting he would murder New York District Attorney, Thomas Dewey, despite orders from Lucky to drop the issue. "Murder Incorporated" members lured Pretty Amberg to a garage where, so fearful that he might survive their murder plot, they shot him, practically skinned him, chopped his limbs off and burned him. Yes, everyone hated Pretty Amberg.

Sam's Restaurant, where the pies are charred in a classic pizza oven built by hand by the family in 1930. Mario (who has been making pies for 59 years there) says that for some good pizza, this is the place, at 238 Court Street, Brooklyn.

Albert Ackalitis

November 12, 1908 - August unknown, 1982

ALBERT ACKALITIS
THE GREEK

Since the turn of the century the docks have always been run by "the mob." This fact has never been a mystery. The first movie to detail this truth was "On The Waterfront" starring our very own film Godfather, Marlon Brando. The film was a blockbuster and it shed light on the stranglehold that the Families had on the docks.

Technically all the five families had a stake in the waterfront, but the Genovese Family seemed to be the most dominant. As far as history is concerned, the docks have been the haven for mob activity going back to Frankie Yale. Frankie, with his pal Al Capone, used to ferry goods through the Brooklyn docks. Their hold on the movement of products from one location to another was due to the "Mafia's" tight grip on the unions.

On the Brooklyn docks, one individual stood out the most; his name was Albert Anastasia. He made sure his policies and rules were always abided by. Albert's role was to collect loans, tap into pension funds and keep a certain order amongst the hard working laborers. Yet he did not do that all alone of course. He did solicit help from his stable of "enforcers."

One such enforcer was Albert "the Greek" Ackalitis. Albert was born on November 12, 1908 and passed away in August of 1982. He lived on Staten Island and Brooklyn. He was one of the premier tough guys on the docks who instilled fear in anyone crossing his or Anastasia's path. A good example was in 1950, a corporation called "Jarka Corp." wanted to work a new pier and needed to assign a pier boss. Jarka was told to hire Tony Anastasio who happened to be Albert Anastasias brother.

The company refused the request. A dock officer named Joe Ryan was approached by Jarka with a complaint, but was told by Joe to hire Tony. Hence, Tony got the job. When all was said and done, the VP of the Jarka Corp. also went ahead and hired Albert Ackalitis. The VP Captain, Douglas Yates made it clear why he hired him, "The guiding thought in hiring Ackalitis," said Captain Yates, "frankly, was to have on that pier some order and discipline, as I call it, amongst the men."

Ryan went further to add "under testimony:" "Because a man's done wrong once, don't show he's a criminal. Why, a man can't get paroled unless somebody'll give him a job." In private, however, the shipowners offered a different rationale. One company official candidly testified that, if given the choice between "hiring a tough ex-convict and a man without a criminal record," he would "take the ex-con ... because if he is in a job as a boss, he'll keep the men in line and get the maximum work out of them, they'll be afraid of him." When another employer was asked why he had hired Albert Ackalitis, a former convict and waterfront tough, he answered: "We would like to have twenty Ackalitises. We get more work out of the man than anybody else. We're not interested in his personal life."

It's not to say that dockworkers were not going to eventually speak their minds. They soon publically began naming names to shed light on the illicit element on the docks. Those names were rattled off in succession: Albert Anastasia and his brothers Anthony and Gerardo, Vincent Mangano, Anthony (Tony Bender) Strollo, Alex (The Ox) Di Brizzi, Toddo Marino, Mickey Bowers, Mickey Clemente, enforcers like "Big John" Ward and Eddie McGrath, Albert Ackalitis and Saro Mogavero. Most of these men were subpoenaed but none of them offered any information.

Albert was the racketeering boss of Pier 18 on the lower westside, and even though he helped Anastasia in Brooklyn, he played a role on many docks. For instance, in New Jersey he was summoned to assist in a dispute. Tony Mike DiLorenzo sought out "Acky's" help with dealing with one, Eddie Florio. He told Albert, 'We got some trouble with Florio, we need to straighten him out."

Ackalitis told Florio that if he did not remove his men off the pier, Albert and his crew would do it their way. Florio acknowledged who Albert was, and succumbed to his demands. Albert asserted his power on the Hudson County Piers from there on.

Albert was also part of what the press called the "Arsenal Gang." They were responsible for the murder of Irish hoodlum Joey Butler. Their hideout was only a few doors from Westside gangster Francis (Two-Gun) Crowley who had it out with the police, before he was subdued. The Arsenal Gang's hideout was discovered by authorities, and what a cache of weapons they found: machine guns, rifles, 10,000 rounds of ammunition, a grenade, pistols and various license plates. Ackalitis had a slew of arrests and was soon on the lam after his last arrest.

Albert would soon face trial for a stabbing and testify in the case and serve time. His toughness was legendary among the Italians and the Irish gangsters but most importantly it was utilized even by the legitimate world of the waterfront.

Unloading coffee beans at the Brooklyn Docks.

Court Pastry Shop which sells traditional Neapolitan and Sicilian cookies. The Zerilli family started the business in 1948 and the sons are still there at 298 Court St. Brooklyn.

Salvatore Musacchio
unknown - unknown

SALVATORE MUSACCHIO
SALLY THE SHEIK

Salvatore "Sally the Sheik" Musacchio operated in a neighborhood and era where everyone knew who the local wiseguys were, what their rank was, and what they did, who ran the ziganette game and who was the shooter. They would never think of relating that information to the authorities and afforded their mobsters the utmost respect. Every morning, the dapper Sheik, in suit, shirt, and tie, who was a captain in the mob family of Joseph Profaci, would parade around one such area, the East New York section of Brooklyn.

During that time he would make a daily stop at "Joe the Barber" shop on Liberty Avenue for a shave. Later, he would enjoy a mid-day meal at Don Peppe restaurant, which he was said to have had a piece of. That restaurant would later move to a location closer to the yet to be born John Gotti's sanctuary area of Ozone Park. For the time being, "Sally the Sheik" lorded over his area in East New York, giving solace and assistance to those who petitioned him and won, and threatening justice to those who broke the "mob's" rules.

One of those who fell under the Sheik's wing was a young Ralph Calletti. In truth, Ralph was the godson of Vito Genovese, a powerful figure in the "family" "Lucky" Luciano had built, and future successor to that group. Genovese eventually became the namesake of that mob family, replacing Luciano and forever solidifying his position as its leader, though in different "families." "Sally the Sheik" and Vito Genovese were close friends. Because of that relationship, the Sheik took it upon himself to look after Vito's godson, Ralph.

One evening, Ralph Calletti, who liked to gamble, got on the wrong side of some bookmakers he owed money to. Their discussion left him with a black eye. The next day, at the barber shop, the Sheik asked him about it. Calletti mumbled some lame excuse and ended by saying "it was nothing." That day, Ralph got a call from his godfather, Vito Genovese, to meet him. Vito showed up with two future bosses of the "Genovese Family," Thomas "Tommy Ryan" Eboli and Vincent "Chin" Gigante. The result was that the bookmaker who had hit Vito's' godson was taken out of a crap game in New Jersey run by another future boss, Jerry Catena. Ralph was given a baseball bat and told to "go to work" on the bookmaker, starting with the shins and knees so he fell to the floor where he was a better target. Ralph Calletti remembered two things about that incident: the sound of bones cracking and not to let "Sally the Sheik" find out anything he didn't want Vito to know.

"Sally the Sheik" was typical of his time, where the wiseguys' world was so all encompassing that they didn't always keep track of things going on in the wider world. One incident that made Ralph laugh was when Sally looked out of the barber shops window and spotted a car parked down the block with two people sitting in the front seat. Sure that they were some arm of law enforcement, he sent one of his bodyguards, Joey Echo, to check them out. Joey returned from his mission to report that the two heads were in fact headrests, which had recently been installed in automobiles. Of course, Ralph and everyone else at "Joe's Barber Shop" laughed after Sally and his men had left.

Within the "Profaci Family," "Sally the Sheik's" position was stronger than just a position earned through deeds. Profaci's brother-in-law, Joseph "The Fat Man" Magliocco, was also the uncle-in-law of Sally's daughter. When Maglioccio was elevated to boss after Joe Profaci died of cancer, he dragged "Sally the Sheik" upstairs with him as underboss. Magliocco, as unfit a boss as could be imagined at the time, allowed Joe Bonnano to talk him into a plot to kill Carlo Gambino and Tommy Lucchese and consolidate the five families under them.

134 - Brooklyn Gangsters

Magliocco gave the assignment to another future boss, Joe Colombo, who, realizing the stupidity of the plot, informed Carlo Gambino. Magliocco was magnanimously allowed to step down instead of being killed. "Sally the Sheik" took over as acting boss. Both he and Maglioccio died of natural causes a short time later, leaving the top spot to Colombo.

The old Barber Shop on Liberty Avenue.

The D'Amico family has been roasting beans and greeting customers at this Carroll Gardens address since 1948, the best coffee in South Brooklyn, 309 Court Street, Brooklyn.

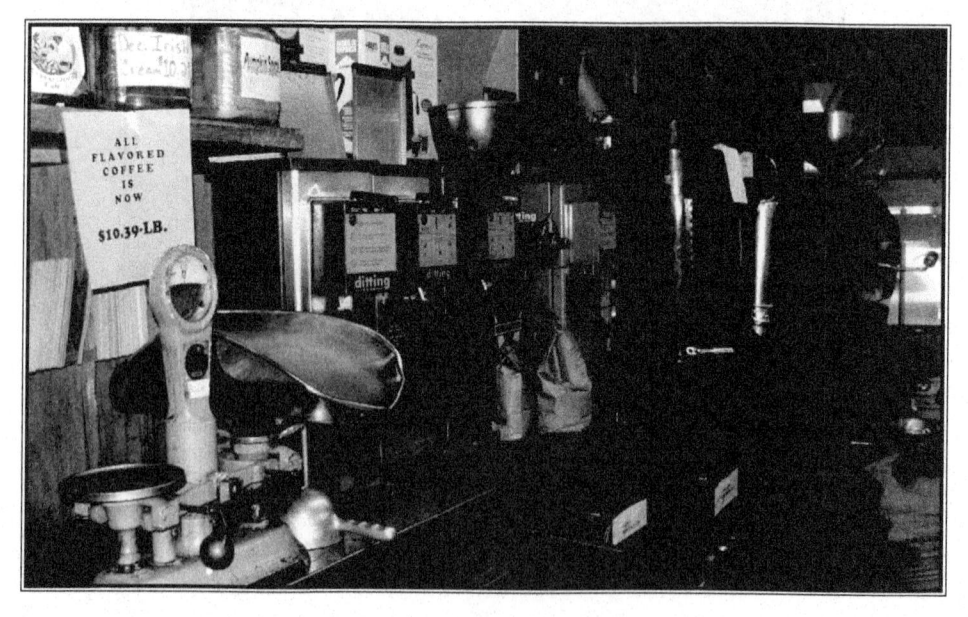

Alphonse Frank Tieri
February 22, 1904 - March 31, 1981

FRANK TIERI
FUNZOUALE

For a period of time in the 1970s, you could not get Pellegrino water, Perrier, or Saratoga water in any Italian restaurant from Little Italy to Bensonhurst. The only "aqua minerale" available was Bella Donna, which tasted as if a dirty mop had been wrung out into its source. Jokes were made about its unpleasant taste, but there were also whispers, words of explanation of why it was the only accompaniment for otherwise good food: "It belongs to Funzouale."

Alphonse Frank "Funzouale" Tieri was the latest street boss of the "Genovese Family," having been anointed after his predecessor "Tommy Ryan" Eboli had died of lead poisoning, not from paint but bullets. "Funzouale" was an older, quieter mob leader in the style of his good friend and boss of another crew, Carlo Gambino. His personal style, however, was different, as he wore custom clothing and could be seen regularly up and down Mulberry Street, sipping espresso at Café Napoli or schmoozing with those diamond and gold purveyors under his command at the jewelry center at 74 Bowery. He could also be seen strolling along Bensonhurt's Bay Parkway, stopping into Alley's or George Richland's men's shops, or on 65th Street in the original Sbarro's and across the street at Cangiano's Pork Store. "Funzouale" was well liked, well respected, and feared.

What made him feared was not a violent temper like Tommy Ryan (when he was a fight manager, Ryan once punched out a referee when he thought his fighter got a bad decision). What made "Funzouale" feared was his "Machiavellian-like" reputation. He had one of his captains murdered. Once that was accomplished, it dawned on him that he hadn't a clue whereto find all the money and businesses this "top earner" had. The only one who might be able to draw him a treasure map was an associate of his departed underling. Instead of working over the deceased captain's man, who claimed he didn't know where any of the "treasure" "Funzouale" sought was, the old man brought him closer into the fold, elevating him to a position as his occasional private chauffeur. One Gambino wiseguy who didn't understand what was going on nearly went through the roof of his Bath Beach social club. The "sometimes" Genovese boss's chauffeur he said, was a rat, who threatened to go to the District Attorney when they were at a sitdown to settle a Gambino-Genovese beef over someone who had given him a bad check in his construction business. None of that seemed to matter to "Funzouale," as it was unthinkable that a Gambino higher up didn't approach him with the story. A year or so later, "Funzouale" shocked everyone by dispensing "goodfella" status on his newfound buddy and sometimes driver. With that done, he told the newly made wiseguy that since they were now bound by a "blood oath" he should share the treasure map he had etched in his brain. Once the man did, "Funzouale" had him murdered. As the Gambino wiseguy had claimed, "Funzouale's" underling was never wiseguy material, but had served an important purpose for the boss of the Genovese Family. (Later, it was claimed that "Funzouale" was merely a street boss and front man for the man pulling the strings, Benny Squints, who was immortalized by Jimmy Breslin in a number of satirical articles about a character he called "Un Occhio, or "One Eye")

Despite a long life of crime and reaching the heights of criminal power, "Funzouale" spent decades between an early arrest in 1924 for armed robbery, when he was twenty years old, and a RICO conviction (the first ever under that statute) and a sentence of ten years in prison in January, 1981. At that time, a bail hearing was held for "Funzouale,' who attended the proceedings in a wheelchair. The old man's lawyers argued for bail, pending an appeal based on the fact that their client was a sick man who had gone through a number of operations, including one for throat cancer. The government argued that it was all an act, and that Tieri should be remanded immediately. While the judge, Thomas P. Griesa, looked like he could go either way, "Funzouale" asked if he could approach the bench and speak with the judge up close, since his voice was little more than a whisper since the operation on his throat. The judge agreed. When "Funzouale" got close enough, he dropped his pants to display a network of scars on his body. Judge Griesa was repulsed, but granted the convicted RICO offender bail. It turned out to be a wise and compassionate decision. Alphonse Frank Tieri, aka "Funzouale," died two months later, on March 31, 1981, of natural causes in Mt. Sinai Hospital.

The original Sbarro's on 65th Street.

Joseph Colombo
December 14, 1914 - May 22, 1978

JOSEPH COLOMBO
JOE

Joseph "Joe" Colombo Sr. (December 14, 1914 - May 22, 1978) ruled over the "Colombo crime family," formerly, the "Profaci family," in Brooklyn, New York. He was 40 years old at the time of his "coronation" in 1963. Colombo, in his day, was the youngest Mafia boss ever. Unfortunately for him, he also was among the small, exclusive clubs, of mob bosses assassinated while in power.

Colombo was an intelligent man of contradictions, best known for siding with Joseph Profaci in his war with the Gallo brothers, and unveiling a plot to take out the Gambino and Lucchese bosses; these efforts led to his taking over the family, which was re-christened in his name.

Colombo is probably best known for his founding of the "Italian-American Civil Rights League." For the honest Italians who supported him and his League in huge numbers, he was a hero who stood up against prejudice against Italians. He even got the word "Mafia" stricken from the script for "The Godfather" film. Some fellow mobsters, including Carlo Gambino, even supported his efforts—at first.

Colombo became a made man in the "Profaci family" in the 1950s. He was charismatic, articulate and respected. Colombo wore $1,000 suits and $500 shoes decades before John Gotti the "Dapper Don" burst on the scene. But beneath the elegant veneer, Colombo was ruggedly built and could turn from a gentleman to a street hood in a heartbeat, as his chosen profession necessitated. Colombo became one of Profaci's main enforcers and quickly proved himself, getting promoted to "capo."

When Profaci died, underboss Giuseppe Magliocco took over as boss and was soon drawn into a plot with "Bonanno crime family" boss Joseph Bonanno, a Profaci confederate, to murder bosses Tommy Lucchese and Carlo Gambino. The plot was planned in retaliation for their support of the Gallos brothers, who were at war with Profaci when he died. Magliocco gave the contracts to Colombo, who promptly revealed the plot to Lucchese and Gambino. "The Commission" eventually forced Bonanno to retire and Magliocco did everyone the favor of quietly dying of cancer.

Magliocco's debt cleared the way for Colombo's rise. Some mobsters resented the ascension of such a young member, but Colombo had the support of "God" in the form of Carlo Gambino, the most powerful boss of any crime family. It was unanimously approved. At the age of 40, Joseph Colombo was boss, the youngest mob boss appointed in America.

In the spring of 1970, Colombo responded to increasing FBI scrutiny of his activities by creating a niche in the civil rights movement for Italian-Americans. It led to the formation of the "Italian-American Civil Rights League," which still exists and is located in Brooklyn, New York.

On June 29, 1970, 150,000 people showed up in Columbus Circle in New York City for the mob-supported "Italian-American Unity Day" rally. Among the participants were five U.S. Congressmen and several prominent entertainers. Under Colombo's guidance, the League went on to develop a national presence. In November 1970, Frank Sinatra himself headlined a benefit for the League at Madison Square Garden.

All this work, of course, brought Colombo increasingly into the limelight. Other mob leaders shunned the publicity like the plague. On June 28, 1971, at the second "Italian Unity Day" rally (by now most other mobsters had pulled away from the League and its activities), Colombo was approaching the podium to address the crowd. Jerome Johnson, a black street hustler, approached Colombo.

Wearing press credentials and disguised as a photojournalist, Johnson fired three shots into Colombo's head. Colombo's men brought Johnson to the ground. A second man stepped out of the crowd, shot Johnson dead and disappeared into the pages of history, never to be indentified. Colombo lingered in a coma for nearly seven years before dying.

The Colombo shooting was never solved. The prime suspect was Joe Gallo, who had alliances with black gangs in Harlem. Gallo resented Colombo, who was allied with Profaci when the Gallo brothers went to war with the family boss over money.

Another suspect was Carlo Gambino, who was angered over the increasing publicity generated by Colombo's activities. At one meeting to discuss these concerns, Colombo allegedly addressed Gambino's complaints by spitting in his face. Additionally, the shooter, Johnson had connections to the Gambino family.

No law enforcement agency ever conducted any investigation into either the Colombo shooting or the Johnson murder.

Columbus Circle

Anthony Augello
unknown - 1982

ATHONY AUGELLO
TONY THE GAWK

Anthony "Tony Gawk" Augello, or "The Gawk," as he was known to friends and law enforcement, was a giant of a man whose handshake reached halfway to an average adult's elbow, in a subculture where most participants were of heights that ranged from short to average. Years ago, many mobsters were suspicious and had trouble trusting anyone over five foot nine or so, unless they personally knew their entire family; anyone over six feet was cause for extra suspicion. Gawk was an exception. He was a proven guy who law enforcement claimed "pissed ice water." Gawk was the guy who knocked a Brazilian diplomat unconscious in a popular Manhattan disco and helped overturn a "Staten Island Advance" news truck when it ran negative articles about his family boss, Joe Colombo. The articles highlighted the Italian American Civil Rights League protest marches in front of the FBI building uptown.

He once stuck up a man making a store's night deposit using his finger as a gun in the man's back and his raspy voice as intimidation. He was so notorious in Brooklyn that when a local bartender, "Eddie Scar," was shot to death, Gawk was arrested and held even though he had been nowhere near the alleged or real scene of the crime (Eddie was killed by a drug dealer in a bar then brought to his apartment building lobby. Shots were fired and the murderer left. Police assumed Eddie had met his end in that lobby on his way home). His typical day would be a trip to "Jasper's" barber shop where he had his hair done every day and "Morris' Luncheonette" where he had his egg white omelets. These routine stops were always "bugged" by law enforcement. If he showed up, nattily dressed, dripping gold and diamonds, and with a pocketful of money to burn at a poker game, a waiting line would form at the table to get a piece of his action.

When doing time in the New York State prison system, Gawk caused so much trouble that guards used to have to handcuff him, strip him naked, and hose him down with icy water in his cell as punishment. One time, when he was incarcerated, he set up a meeting with the FBI to discuss "rolling over" and changing sides. At that time for wise-guys at that "pre-Sammy the Bull period," was the exception rather than the rule, as the latter is today. Tony's lawyer, Ira Cooper, who was also one of mine, was in shock. Could it be that one of the toughest guys he knew would become a rat? He went to the interview with a heavy heart. Gawk got everyone together in a big courthouse conference room: the two Assistant U.S. Attorneys for the Eastern District of New York who were handling his case, FBI Agents, our aforementioned attorney, and last but not least the court stenographer he insisted on.

As Cooper related to me afterward, Tony made sure the stenographer was ready to take down everything he said, then went about telling prosecutors and agents how he had sex with their mothers and sisters at various times in the past. The first reaction was shock. Everyone sat there, not able to absorb what they were hearing. Once recovered, they dragged him out of the room and practically had to carry the flabbergasted attorney out on a stretcher.

But Gawkie had two major mob problems. First, he was terrible at "sit-downs" with other mob guys. He had an uncanny ability to snatch defeat from the jaws of victory. He knew it too and sometimes begged off with a feigned illness, so someone else could represent his side, and was usually surprised if they won. More important, and ultimately deadly, he was scared to death of his bosses. He'd actually get physically sick...no faking...if he got called downtown by higher ups.

Then he screwed up and got in trouble for drug dealing that mandated a death sentence for anyone in his crew. He had befriended a black drug dealer in prison, who offered him a deal when they both hit Brooklyn streets. No one knew what he was up to. When the arrest came, no one could believe that he would take a chance like that. Also, once the arrest came, he knew his fate. Was Gawk worried about dying? Yes and no.

No one of any sense wants to die. However, what worried him most was that if he was killed and his body never found, the properties and cash that his family and friends had put up for his bail would be forfeited. He also had real pressure from the Feds, since he already owed them parole time for an extortion sentence he had done. Couldn't rat; couldn't hide. What to do, what to do? Gawk decided that the best thing was to go to a "McDonald's" parking lot pay phone, call some friends to say goodbye, then blow his brains out with a .357 Magnum on the spot. Remaining loyal to his superiors to the end, Tony Gawk even left a note that solely blamed FBI pressure for his suicide. His last words on the phone, "Tell everyone the Gawk is still an honorable guy."

I had the pleasure of meeting "Tony The Gawk" many years ago. My father and I used to meet Tony once a week at "Jasper's Barber" shop on Avenue U in Brooklyn. He was a big, rough, cigar-smoking guy you wouldn't want to fuck with. R.I.P.

A 357 Magnum

Richard Pagliarulo
unknown - unknown

RICHARD PAGLIARULO
LITTLE RICHIE / THE WIG

Richard Pagliarulo was a person at war with himself, at war with who he believed he was, and how he was accepted, or not, by others important to him. The root of his problem began before he was born, when his future father's sister married a soon to be well known mobster, Larry Gallo. As he grew up, he also grew to love and idolize his legendary uncle, and ultimately prove himself worthy of being a member of his crew. Richie was not "The Wig" then, just "Little Richie"; he still had hair, much of which he lost as a result of a nasty head wound sustained when he was a passenger in a car being chased by police. If Richie hadn't had much too much to drink and was not too limp to be tossed around like a rag doll, he would have probably lost his life along with his hair.

In an effort to prove himself, he often did bizarre things. For example, he would leave his girlfriend sitting alone at the bar in a club where his uncle's crew hung out. If a guy approached his girl, "Little Richie" would rush over and, without a word, knock the guy out cold. For a little man, no more than 5'5", he packed a giant's punch. He wasn't known for a having a great mind, but certainly had "balls," and proved it on a number of occasions.

His world began to unravel when his uncle Larry Gallo died of natural causes at only forty-one years old. Instead of being embraced, Richie found himself on the outs with those members of the crew that hadn't transferred over to other groups within the "Colombo Family." He wasn't accepted the same way as he was when "Uncle" was alive. The King was dead; long live the King. All the promises his uncle had made for his future were gone.

After a few years of ups and downs and a couple of murders surrounding him, and deaths of close associates, he landed with Anthony "Tony Gawk" Augello. For political and some financial considerations, "Gawk" kept Richie off the record, never officially listing him as an underling of his with the family bosses. That worked for Richie for awhile. He was a good earner and wasn't a big spender or an extravagant dresser and didn't live lavishly. Because he wasn't on record with the "Gawk" and didn't have the flash that drew attention, he was able to exist in the mob world and also hang on to a lot of his money that "higher ups" would have taken in taxes.

However, once again, Richie lost a "rabbi." Tony Gawk, pressured by the FBI and his bosses after a drug arrest, blew his brains out at the payphone in a McDonald's parking lot. When family "higher ups" wanted to know what was going on, and wanted to assign some of Tony's men to "Benny the Sidge," fellow mobster Patty Catalano asked others that knew of Richie's status not to mention him. He said that he could move Richie quietly to the Lucchese crew, where he would be treated better and have a real chance to be "made." Little did Patty know that his good intentions were actually signing a death warrant for Richie Pagliarulo.

As intended, Richie wound up with the "Lucchese crew," and eventually became a right hand shooter for his boss, Anthony "Gaspipe" Casso. When "Gaspipe" began murdering everyone he dreamed might betray him (and it was in madman numbers) Richie started dropping bodies for him all over the place. It never dawned on Richie that the numbers were becoming bizarre, and that getting rid of Casso would have ended the fratricide. He just kept shooting, piling up bodies for a pat on the head from a guy who would soon become a government witness. When, after being arrested for carrying out a good part of "Gaspipe's" bloody rampage, Richie was offered a plea where he would have a chance to see daylight sometime in his life, he refused, and insisted on going to trial. He was convicted in a matter of a few hours. According to "Gangbusters," by Ernest Volkman, when Judge Nickerson sentenced Richie, he prefaced the sentencing by mentioning that the defendant had been convicted of forty-eight murders. Richie interrupted the judge by correcting the number as "forty-nine." He got life. Again, he proved he had more "balls than brains."

Once in prison, it dawned on the forty-something year old, that he would never see the street again. He started coming apart at the seams, writing letters that seemed unrealistic and unfocused. Richie didn't fully bust a seam, but his heart did. If there were an organization for "dumb," just those last acts for "Gaspipe," and the correction in front of the judge would have made him its poster boy. R.I.P.

Larry Gallo, Little Richie's uncle.

20's Flapper style dress.

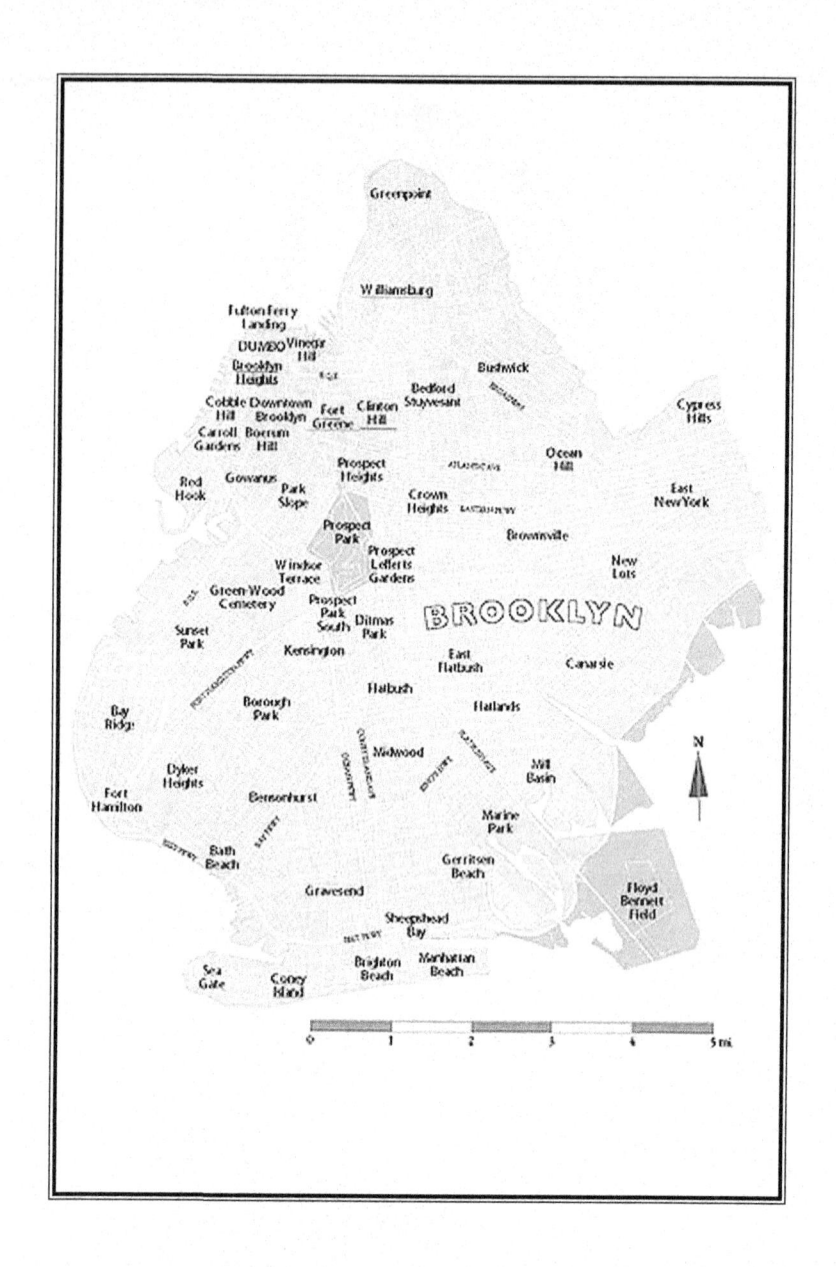

MOB CANDY
70 SQAURE MILES OF BLOOD AND BALLS

150 - Brooklyn Gangsters